KINGDOM MEN RISING

TONY EVANS

Lifeway Press®
Nashville, Tennessee

EDITORIAL TEAM

Heather Hair
Writer

Kyle Wiltshire
Content Editor

Brooke Hill
Production Editor

Jon Rodda
Art Director

Karen Daniel
Editorial Team Leader

John Paul Basham
Manager, Student Ministry Publishing

Ben Trueblood
Director, Student Ministry

ISBN 978-1-0877-5779-7 • Item 005836223

DEWEY: 248.842

Subhead: RELIGION / CHRISTIAN MINISTRY / YOUTH

My deepest thanks go to Mrs. Heather Hair for her skills and insights in collaboration on this manuscript.

To order additional copies of this resource, write to Lifeway Resources Customer Service; One Lifeway Plaza; Nashville, TN 37234; fax 615-251-5933; call toll free 800-458-2772; order online at Lifeway.com; or email orderentry@lifeway.com.

Printed in the United States of America

Student Ministry Publishing • Lifeway Resources • One Lifeway Plaza • Nashville, TN 37234

CONTENTS

ABOUT THE AUTHOR

DR. TONY EVANS is one of the country's most respected leaders in evangelical circles. He is a pastor, best-selling author, and frequent speaker at Bible conferences and seminars throughout the nation.

Dr. Evans has served as the senior pastor of Oak Cliff Bible Fellowship for over forty-five years, witnessing its growth from ten people in 1976 to now over ten thousand congregants with over one hundred ministries.

Dr. Evans also serves as president of The Urban Alternative, a national ministry that seeks to restore hope and transform lives through the proclamation and application of the Word of God. His daily radio broadcast, The Alternative with Dr. Tony Evans, can be heard on over 1,400 radio outlets throughout the United States and in more than 130 countries.

Dr. Evans holds the honor of writing and publishing the first full-Bible commentary and study Bible by an African American. The study Bible and commentary went on to sell more than 225,000 copies in the first year.

Dr. Evans is the former chaplain for the Dallas Cowboys and the Dallas Mavericks.

Through his local church and national ministry, Dr. Evans has set in motion a kingdom agenda philosophy of ministry that teaches God's comprehensive rule over every area of life as demonstrated through the individual, family, church, and society.

Dr. Evans was married to Lois, his wife and ministry partner of over 50 years, until Lois transitioned to glory in late 2019. They are the proud parents of four, grandparents of thirteen, and great-grandparents of three.

HOW TO GET THE MOST FROM THIS STUDY

This Bible study book includes eight weeks of content for group and personal study.

GROUP SESSIONS

Regardless of what day of the week your group meets, each week of content begins with a group session. Each group session uses the following format to facilitate meaningful interaction among group members, with God's Word, and with the video teaching.

START. This page includes questions to get the conversation started and to introduce the video teaching.

WATCH. This page includes key points from the video teaching so that participants can follow along as they watch the video. Video sessions are available at lifeway.com/kingdommenrising. Make sure your select the student version of the videos.

MAN UP. This page includes questions and statements that guide the group to respond to the video teaching and to relevant Bible passages.

PERSONAL STUDY

Each week provides three days of Bible study and learning activities for individual engagement between group sessions: "Hit the Streets" and two Bible studies.

HIT THE STREETS. This section highlights practical steps for taking the week's teaching and putting it into practice.

BIBLE STUDIES. These personal studies revisit stories, Scriptures, and themes introduced in the videos so that guys can understand and apply them on a personal level. Guys should use the other days of the week to reflect on what God is teaching them and to practice putting the Biblical principles into action.

D-GROUP GUIDES

In addition to the group sessions and personal studies, D-Group guides are provided in the back of this Bible study book. These guides correspond to the eight weeks of study and are designed to be used in a smaller group of three or four guys for deeper discussion and accountability. Each week includes a guide for smaller-group discussion. Each guide provides helpful thoughts on the week's content and suggests a few questions for discussion by and accountability among the group.

TIPS FOR LEADING A SMALL GROUP

Follow these guidelines to prepare for each group session.

PRAYERFULLY PREPARE

REVIEW. Review the weekly material and group questions ahead of time. Videos are available at lifeway.com/kingdommenrising.

PRAY. Be intentional about praying for each person in the group.

Ask the Holy Spirit to work through you and the group discussion as you point to Jesus each week through God's Word.

MINIMIZE DISTRACTIONS

Create an environment that doesn't distract. Ask students not to use their phones and to bring a physical Bible. Plan ahead by considering these details, including seating, temperature, lighting, snacks, and general cleanliness. While most young men aren't terribly concerned with these things (other than snacks), it will help them not be distracted. Do everything in your ability to help students focus on what's most important: connecting with God, the Bible, and each other.

ENCOURAGE DISCUSSION

A good small-group experience has the following characteristics.

EVERYONE IS INCLUDED. Your goal is to foster a community in which guys are welcome just as they are but encouraged to grow spiritually. Always be aware of opportunities to include any students who visit the group and to invite new guys to join your group.

EVERYONE PARTICIPATES. Encourage everyone to ask questions, share responses, or read aloud.

NO ONE DOMINATES—NOT EVEN THE LEADER. Be sure that your time speaking as a leader takes up less than half of your time together as a group. Politely guide discussion if anyone dominates or gets off track theologically.

NOBODY IS RUSHED THROUGH QUESTIONS. Don't feel that a moment of silence is a bad thing. Students often need time to think about their responses to questions they've just heard or to gain courage to share what God is stirring in their hearts.

INPUT IS AFFIRMED AND FOLLOWED UP. Make sure you point out something true or helpful in a response. Don't just move on. Build community with follow-up questions, asking how other people have experienced similar things or how a truth has shaped their understanding of God and the Scripture you're studying. People are less likely to speak up if they fear that you don't actually want to hear their answers or that you're looking for only a certain answer.

GOD AND HIS WORD ARE CENTRAL. Opinions and experiences can be helpful, but God has given us the truth. Trust God's Word to be the authority and God's Spirit to work in people's lives. You can't change anyone, but God can. Continually point students to the Word and to active steps of faith.

KEEP CONNECTING

Think of ways to connect with students during the week. Participation during the group session is always improved when guys spend time connecting with one another outside the group sessions. The more people are comfortable with and involved in one another's lives, the more they'll look forward to being together. When people move beyond being friendly to truly being friends who form a community, they come to each session eager to engage instead of just attending.

ENCOURAGE STUDENTS with thoughts, commitments, or questions from the session by connecting through texts, social media, and school visits (where permissible).

BUILD DEEPER FRIENDSHIPS by planning or spontaneously inviting group members to join you outside your regularly scheduled group time for activities like meals, fun activities, and projects around your school, church, or community.

And if you belong to Christ, then you are Abraham's descendants, heirs according to promise.

GALATIANS 3:29

WEEK 1
CHOSEN FOR THE CHALLENGE

KINGDOM MEN RISING

START

Welcome to group session 1 of *Kingdom Men Rising*.

As an illustration, find some Legos or building blocks from the church nursery and build two small structures. Show your group how important a strong foundation is with these building materials. Build something with an unstable foundation and show how easily it falls. Then build something with a strong foundation and show how much more difficult it is to bring it down.

Why is it so important to have a strong foundation when building something?

At this point in your life, you may not know much about construction. But, as you've seen and probably already know, to build anything that lasts, you have to have a strong foundation to build upon. Foundations aren't meant to be pretty or showy; they're meant to be sturdy, solid, stable, and strong. In fact, we typically only talk about foundations when a problem arises that needs to be looked at and addressed.

What happens when a building is constructed on top of a bad foundation?

God created you with a foundation in mind. Your role on earth isn't to draw attention to yourself or be as showy as you can be. God has placed you in a position to one day provide the support, stability, and strength needed to build healthy communities and families. That's not where you are now as a young man, but what you do today helps create the foundation you'll build upon as you grow into a man.

God hasn't just called you to be a man. He's called you to be a man focused on His kingdom. A kingdom man. As a kingdom man, God has given you a purpose to live out and a divine design to fulfill. This session speaks to your unique calling to provide the foundational framework upon which your influence can rest and rise.

Ask someone to pray before watching the video teaching.

Chosen for the Challenge
WATCH

Use this space to take notes during the video teaching.

MAN UP

Use the following questions to discuss the video teaching.

Read Genesis 18:19 together.

For I have chosen him, so that he may command his children and his household after him to keep the way of the LORD by doing righteousness and justice, so that the LORD may bring upon Abraham what He has spoken about him.
Genesis 18:19

Name some of the things God promised to Abraham. See Genesis 12:2-3 for some help.

When God called Abraham, He told him that He had chosen him. He promised to make Abraham's name great and his descendants many. He chose to bless Abraham in order to bless others. God made these promises to Abraham so that ultimately, we might be blessed through our relationship with one of Abraham's descendants.

Read Galatians 3:29 together.

And if you belong to Christ, then you are Abraham's descendants, heirs according to promise.
Galatians 3:29

What does it mean to be an heir? Who is a example of an heir that you know of in our society today?

In what ways have Abraham's promises been passed down to you?

What responsibilities do we have because of the promises that have been given to us?

Once we give our lives to Jesus, He lays claim to us, and that means we have a position to play on a bigger team. We've been given a blessing that God expects us to pass on to others. In other words, we're a part of a kingdom team. We've been called to take our stand with God, for God, from God, and about God, in a world that needs to know God.

Why does following God compel us to take a stand for Him?

Describe one way you have taken a stand for God recently. What did you learn from that experience? How were others impacted?

The blessing God gives us is meant to extend beyond us. One way to take a stand for God is to intentionally inject your life into the lives of others. This is done through discipleship. At this point in your life, you may not feel equipped to disciple someone else. That doesn't mean you can't share what God has taught you with others. You don't have to have graduated with a degree in Biblical Studies to do this. All you have to do is open yourself up to what God wants to do in you and trust Him to lead you.

The truth is, you need someone pouring into you. No matter your age, all guys need godly examples of men to follow. We all need wise counsel and to have men in our lives who know and love God to teach us how we can know and love God more.

What are some common hesitations guys have when it comes to committing to disciple someone else or be discipled by someone else?

Can you share a personal example of the result of having been discipled at some point in your life? If you do not have a personal example, share a hope you would expect to see as a result of being discipled by someone else.

PRAYER

Father, make us intentional about standing up for You and fulfilling the role You have for us. Help us be people of our word. Lay down in us Your truth, wisdom, and grace so that we may have a solid foundation to build our lives upon. Open up opportunities for us to be discipled and give us the chance to help others grow in their spiritual maturity as well. In the name of Jesus, amen.

HIT THE STREETS

GOD'S MEET UP

Three times a year, God called the men of Israel to gather together and meet with Him through yearly festivals. Participating in the worship of God would define their identities and give them instructions for how to follow Him.

> *Three times a year all your males are to appear before the Lord*
> *GOD, the God of Israel. For I will drive out nations before you and*
> *enlarge your borders, and no man shall covet your land when you go*
> *up three times a year to appear before the LORD your God.*
> **Exodus 34:23-24**

God let the men know when they came before Him that if they obeyed Him and submitted to His authority, then He would bless them, their families, and their nation. Specifically, God made three promises to protect them as they committed themselves to seeking the Lord. Let's take a deeper look at each of these three promises.

DRIVE OUT NATIONS BEFORE YOU

The promise to drive out nations before them was a promise of security. Enemy nations could only mean one thing: instability. While following God and seeking Him does not mean that our lives will always be easy, they will be secure in His grasp.

In what ways have you witnessed God bring stability and calm to your life as you follow Him?

2 ENLARGE YOUR BORDERS

When God promises to enlarge our borders, He is referring to that space where you carry influence and impact. This could mean your friendships, relationships, the teams you play on, the activities you participate in, or even the hobbies you love to do. Enlarging our boarders is meant to impact His kingdom, not ours.

How can you spread God's goodness and love in the places where He has given you influence and impact?

3 ALLOW NO MAN TO COVET YOUR LAND

In these verses, God was making a promise that when these men left their homes to attend festivals to worship and honor God, no one would take what belonged to them. For you, it means that you can trust God with all that He has entrusted to you.

Why is it important to rest in the truth of God's protection with regard to what He has given you?

Father, all three of these promises from You point to one truth: we can trust You with everything. You are faithful. You are good. You are love. Help us to know this and believe this with all of our hearts so that we can help others know it and believe it, too. In the name of Jesus, amen.

DAY 2
JUMP, OR BE JUMPED

A checker, or the round piece that is used to play the game checkers, has two sides. One side has a crown on it, and the other does not. That is because each checker was created to become a king. A checker is crowned when it has successfully made it to the other side of the board. After that point, it will have the ability to maneuver and function at a much higher level than it could prior to being crowned.

The reality is that most individual checkers will not successfully make it to the other end of the board because the opposition will jump them and knock them out of the game. Whether a checker achieves its created goal of being crowned as a king is fully determined by the hand controlling it.

When God created men, He created them under His authority. However, ever since the first man, Adam, Satan has sought to "jump" men to keep them from fulfilling their kingdom purposes. He goes to great lengths to keep us from functioning in alignment with God so that our lives and everything around us experience the consequences and confusion of us living independently from God. We must live as we were created: under God's authority. When we follow Him, we have the ability to be like a king in checkers. We can jump and not be jumped by Satan's attacks.

Read 1 Peter 5:8-9 and Ephesians 4:26-27 and answer the following questions.

*Be sober-minded, be alert. Your adversary the devil is prowling around
like a roaring lion, looking for anyone he can devour. Resist him,
firm in the faith, knowing that the same kind of sufferings are being
experienced by your fellow believers throughout the world.*
1 Peter 5:8-9 (CSB)

*Be angry, and yet do not sin; do not let the sun go down on
your anger, and do not give the devil an opportunity.*
Ephesians 4:26-27

What are some ways we can resist Satan's attempt to "jump" us?

Describe in your own words what it means to live "sober-minded" and to always "be alert" for Satan's schemes.

Satan is free to roam, but God has him on a leash. Yet God will often allow Satan to tempt us, or wage war against us, because it is during these times of testing that our true character is either formed or revealed.

The strength we need to successfully do battle with the devil is supplied by God (see Eph. 6:10-11). That may seem obvious, but judging from the way we treat this truth, it bears repeating.

Many of us tend to swing toward one of two extremes when it comes to the devil. Sometimes we overestimate him. We become fearful and timid, hoping to keep Satan from leaping upon us. Others times we underestimate him. Yes, Satan is a defeated foe, but even though he is nothing more than a condemned death row inmate awaiting execution, it's not wise to sleep in his cell.

Mark your own perspective of Satan on the chart where 1 means you overestimate him and 10 means you underestimate him:

1   2   3   4   5   6   7   8   9   10

Why is it critical to have a healthy understanding of Satan's strategies and strengths in order to defeat him?

How should your understanding of Satan and his goals affect your decisions?

The inability or even unwillingness to wage war against the enemy in our lives has kept too many of us in a cycle of defeat, discouragement, confusion, rebellion, and addiction. As a result, we face spiritual, social, physical, and emotional chaos in our lives. Too many of us have become weak and passive or arrogant and prideful, leaving our lives in dysfunction or ruin.

Yet, despite all we see around us and the turmoil we my feel in our lives, there remains hope. God created us to be kingdom men who pursue an intimate relationship with Him while simultaneously representing Him in all we do. God desires for us to rise to the challenge we were chosen for and accept the responsibility of pursuing Him in our lives, resisting the devil and chasing hard after God.

Just as the first Adam brought defeat to the human race, the last Adam, Jesus Christ, came to bring victory (see 1 Cor. 15:22). It's time for us, under the lordship of Jesus Christ, to change the trajectory of our lives as we submit ourselves to Him and His kingdom agenda.

God's kingdom agenda is "the visible manifestation of the comprehensive rule of God over every area of life." Rephrase this in your own words.

Give an example of submitting yourself to Christ and His kingdom agenda.

How might your submission enable you to defeat the enemy's plans in your life?

If and when we decide to rise up to fulfill our calling, we will see God heal our hearts. This will affect our schools, teams, clubs, churches, neighborhoods, familes, and relationships. We will see victory over Satan and his strategies. This study is a call to those of us who long to see what God will do with the awakening of His own disciples who will then lead others to infiltrate the culture as kingdom citizens. Once we learn how to wage our own battles in order to wear our own crowns, we can then be used by God to crown others with kingdom values as well. We were chosen for this challenge by God Himself.

Read Judges 17:6 and answer the following questions.

In those days there was no king in Israel; every man
did what was right in his own eyes.

Judges 17:6

What happens when everyone does what they think is right in their own eyes?

How have you seen this happen in our world today?

How has this kind of thinking ultimately hurt people?

List one practical thing you can do this week in your circle of influence in order to guide others toward God's set standards. (Be creative—this could mean in your school, at home, at church, on social media, or also in your prayer time).

Pray about one area in your life where you need to step up your game against Satan's schemes. Look for open doors that Satan is using to get into your life. Ask God how you can close these doors to the enemy. Also, spend some time in prayer asking for God's wisdom regarding His standards and desires for all people's lives. Ask Him to reveal where your standards are not up to par with His so you can adjust and be in alignment with Him.

DAY 3
CALLED TO BE A KINGDOM MAN

A kingdom man may be defined as:

> A man who visibly and consistently submits to the comprehensive relationship and rule of God, underneath the lordship of Jesus Christ, in every area of life.

You can sum it up in one short statement: a kingdom man accepts his responsibilities under God and faithfully carries them out. As he walks in faithfulness, God moves to support him in doing God's kingdom business. When he is unfaithful, Satan steals the show. God has called every Christian man, young and old, to be a kingdom man.

Notice in the definition of a kingdom man, the word "consistently" is used rather than "perfectly." What does it look like to "consistently" live out a life of submission under God, especially in those times when you fall short?

Why is it spiritually dangerous to make excuses for your failures rather than accept responsibility for where you may have dropped the ball?

Consider a football team. When a player makes a mistake, it is common for that player to pat himself on his chest as a way of indicating that he knows it was his fault. It's a nonverbal way of saying, "Sorry guys, let's try again. That one was on me." The other players will nod or pat him on his shoulder and encourage him to do better next time. This type of honest awareness and self-evaluation allows players to stay connected as a team while pursuing a shared goal. Our goal is consistency, not perfection.

How does taking personal ownership of our failures impact others?

In what ways can you take greater personal responsibility for mistakes or issues in your own life? In your friendships?

Have you ever had a relationship with someone who consistently blamed someone else for his or her own mistakes? What did this pattern do to the relationships around him or her?

God calls each of us to own our failures and be authentic about our mistakes. Living as kingdom men requires submission, which is consistency coupled with humility. This type of spirit creates an atmosphere of mutual respect, transparency, and grace where great things can be accomplished for God, individually and collectively.

Each of us has been created by God with a specific position to fill and a purpose to live out. He has scouted, pursued, and drafted you for His kingdom team. Our culture wants to give us tons of other reasons for being a man, but God created us for greatness in His kingdom.

Read Genesis 18:17-19a and Galatians 3:16,29, then answer the following questions.

The LORD said, "Shall I hide from Abraham what I am about to do, since Abraham will surely become a great and mighty nation, and in him all the nations of the earth will be blessed? For I have chosen him …"
Genesis 18:17-19a

Now the promises were spoken to Abraham and to his seed. He does not say, "And to seeds," as one would in referring to many, but rather as in referring to one, "And to your seed," that is, Christ.
Galatians 3:16

And if you belong to Christ, then you are Abraham's descendants, heirs according to promise.
Galatians 3:29

How have you seen God bless others through you?

What habits, attitudes, or lifestyles need to change in you for you to continue to be a blessing to others in the future?

Abraham's promise is ours through Jesus. It's yours. Own it. Abraham's faith led to the blessing of untold millions for thousands of years after his death. Like Abraham, you are meant to pass your blessing onto others. To embrace God's promise naturally includes influencing all those around you. When you think of Michael Jordan or LeBron James, you don't just think of somebody who played basketball. You think of someone who influenced the entire game of basketball and their teams. Why? Because they left their mark. Their mere presence elevated the players around them, and as a result, all were able to achieve more individually and collectively than many thought they ever would. We are to do the same.

Describe a man you know who "influences" and "elevates" the lives of others simply by who he is and what he does.

How can you position yourself to be used by God in "elevating" the lives of those within your circle of influence?

Some of you who have decided to participate in this Bible study may be at a place where you have made mistakes, you live with regret, or you have simply failed to maximize the gifts and skills God has given you. It could be that life hasn't been fair. You may want to embrace God's calling on your life, but you just don't know how you could possibly get there with all that is missing or messed up in your life.

If that's you, remember that success from God's perspective has more to do with heart than skill, just as success in so many areas of life has more to do with effort than talent. Those who put in the work rise to the top. Those who don't most often remain at the bottom or like a tire stuck in the mud, spinning but going nowhere.

Tom Brady didn't get drafted until the sixth round, but he went on to win seven Super Bowl championships. Brady didn't allow his draft status to determine the effort he put into the game. This principle ought to ring true for kingdom men as well. It is your willingness to show up in life day in and day out, be present in relationships, put forth the effort, commit, give, apply diligence, study the Word, and invest in others that will shape your own legacy of distinction. God loves to use those who want to be used by Him. He consistently blesses those who consistently pursue Him.

Kingdom men do three things:

Show up. Be present. Stay consistent.

If you do those three things, you will leave a legacy of excellence. After all, legacy is the culmination of a million middle moments done well. It's not about that Hail Mary or kickoff return for a touchdown. It's the small things—the consistent conversations and wise choices that add up over time. That's what creates the heritage you leave behind.

**Legacy is "the culmination of a million middle moments done well."
What practical steps can you take this week to focus more on the
"middle moments" of life and investing in those around you?**

You are called to a life of greatness and purpose in God's kingdom. But greatness is created day in and day out when you show up and invest in the lives of others. It also requires that you be diligent in keeping your own spiritual muscles strong by seeking God above all else and embracing the calling and promises in His Word.

Pray for the discipline you need to live consistently as a kingdom man. Ask God to provide the structure in your life that will enable you to focus more fully on Him and His call for you. If you are in need of encouragement, take a moment to look around you and consider the impact you have had on others for good and God's kingdom. If you are unable to recognize anything, ask the Spirit to reveal it to you; then build on that success every moment of every day moving forward.

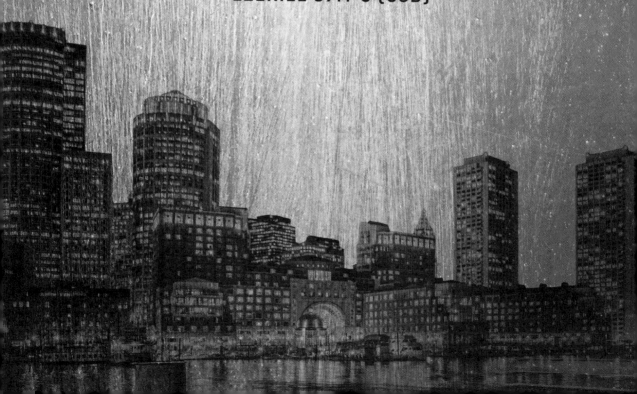

The hand of the Lord was on me, and he brought me out by his Spirit and set me down in the middle of the valley; it was full of bones. He led me all around them. There were a great many of them on the surface of the valley, and they were very dry. Then he said to me, "Son of man, can these bones live?" I replied, "Lord God, only you know."

EZEKIEL 37:1-3 (CSB)

WEEK 2
DRY BONES DANCING

START

Welcome to group session 2 of *Kingdom Men Rising.*

Last week we talked about being chosen for the challenge to live as a young kingdom man. We saw the kind of person God wants us to be and were challenged to extend our influence and impact for the glory of God.

Share one way you were encouraged by last week's session.

This week we will learn to overcome Satan's distractions and trust in God's plans, purposes, and promises for us. As an illustration, search YouTube for "Duke Speedo Guy" and share the video with your group. Many people will go to great lengths to distract the opposing team at the freethrow line, but this guy might have taken it to the extreme, even if he accomplished his goal.

Describe other strategies home team fans use to distract the opposing team when they're trying to shoot a freethrow, make a call, or run a play.

In what ways does Satan seek to distract us from hearing clearly from God?

When an opposing team takes to the field or court, the home team fans will often yell loudly in order to keep the opposing team from hearing the play being called. In this way, they seek to disrupt the play and create a home field/court advantage.

Satan uses a similar strategy in our lives by putting distractions into our hearts and minds so that we cannot hear clearly from God. Due to this effective approach, too many of us remain down when we should be up, defeated when we should be winning, and lost when we should know the way to go. God is calling to each of us loudly and clearly. It is up to us to focus and look past the distractions to what He has to say.

Ask someone to pray before watching the video teaching.

Dry Bones Dancing

WATCH

Use this space to take notes during the video teaching.

MAN UP

Use the following questions to discuss the video teaching.

When you leave your house and go somewhere else, you'll notice a common occurance. Your phone will no longer be able to find the signal for your home wifi router. But when you come back, you'll pick up that signal again because you're home.

Read Isaiah 64:4 together.

For from days of old they have not heard or perceived by ear, Nor has the eye seen a God besides You, Who acts in behalf of the one who waits for Him.
Isaiah 64:4

Why do you think those who did not hear, as referenced in Isaiah 64:4, could not discern or perceive God's voice?

In what ways is this lack of hearing evident in our world today?

How does proximity to God increase our ability to hear from Him?

Far too many of us have left home. We've left our commitment to God and have committed to our culture instead. Yet we still wonder why we're in a dry place and we're not picking up heaven's signal anymore. To hear from heaven, we need to leave the dry place far away from home and trust in the God who breathes life where there appears to be none.

Read Ezekiel 37:1-3 together.

The hand of the Lord was on me, and he brought me out by his Spirit and set me down in the middle of the valley; it was full of bones. He led me all around them. There were a great many of them on the surface of the valley, and they were very dry. Then he said to me, "Son of man, can these bones live?" I replied, "Lord God, only you know."
Ezekiel 37:1-3 (CSB)

When Ezekiel was faced with the question of if the dry bones could live, he gave the answer many of us need to give today—"God, only You know. I can't answer that question because stuff looks so bad, and we're in such a mess, and things are so divided, and the chaos is so overwhelming." In other words, if this is going to be fixed, God has to fix it.

What areas of our culture today—either the church culture or the culture at large—appear to be beyond fixing from a human perspective?

Describe a time where you felt like you had no solution to the problem at hand, yet you witnessed God come through to turn it around.

The account of Ezekiel and the dry bones lying dead on the valley floor reflect what many of us sense in our lives during trials and difficulties. We feel like there is no way out of our slumber, struggling, and stumbling. Yet God will do everything He has purposed and promised in His Word.

If we're going to become the men God has created us to be, we have to trust God's power. God has spoken, and He does not stutter. When we trust Him and embrace the promises from His Word, He can redeem any difficulty and cause the dry bones of our dire circumstances to get up and dance again.

If we have God's promises and know God's power, why do we often fail to trust them when life gets difficult?

What promises of God do you believe we need to trust in today?

What promises do you need to trust in personally?

PRAYER

Father, make us men who hear You clearly. Remove the distractions so that we can discern Your voice. Help us identify the things in our lives that are keeping us from truly turning to You and understanding the truths You've outlined for us in Your Word. In the name of Jesus, amen.

HIT THE STREETS

GOD'S WORD AND SPIRIT

In October 2018, the Soyuz MS-10 rocket failed to reach the International Space Station. Take a moment and consider how to prevent another malfunction like this from happening again. Get as detailed in your solution as you need to be.

This was a trick question. You may have heard of this incident, but you don't know anything about what happened or why. It's hard to fix a problem when you don't know anything about the cause. Whenever you are looking for a solution to a problem, you must address the cause. Far too many people are doing patchwork on symptoms rather than dealing with the systemic roots that have led to the decay in our world. If we are ever going to get things right, we have to address the spiritual causes beneath the brokenness we are experiencing.

God has given us two key methods for curing what ails us. He has provided two critical components we must apply in order to rise up from the ashes of decay. Both of these principles were given to Ezekiel when he stood in the valley of dead, dry bones.

1 RETURN TO GOD'S WORD.

He said to me, "Prophesy concerning these bones and say to them: Dry bones, hear the word of the Lord! This is what the Lord God says to these bones: I will cause breath to enter you, and you will live."

Ezekiel 37:4-5 (CSB)

If you're dry—spiritually, emotionally, relationally, or in any other way—it is most likely because you are distant from God and His Word. Spending regular and unhurried time in God's Word is essential for spiritual life and growth.

When will you spend time with God daily? Draft a battle plan. Set a time and a place. Write down your approach here.

2 RECEIVE A FRESH ENCOUNTER WITH GOD'S SPIRIT.

He said to me, "Prophesy to the breath, prophesy, son of man. Say to it: This is what the Lord God says: Breath, come from the four winds and breathe into these slain so that they may live!" So I prophesied as he commanded me; the breath entered them, and they came to life and stood on their feet, a vast army.

Ezekiel 37:9-10 (CSB)

After the truth of His Word was given to the dry bones in the valley, God then gave them the power of His Spirit. The original Hebrew word translated as "breath" in verse nine is the word God used to identify His Spirit at the beginning of the creation process in Genesis 1:2. With His Spirit, God breathed new life into the dead bones. Through this combination of the Word and the Spirit, God awakened lifeless bones.

List three practical ways you can connect more authentically with the Holy Spirit. Seek to apply these three ways every day this week, then come back and describe what impact that had on your life.

Father, breathe fresh life into me. Help me to trust Your Word and obey it. Help me to address the issues that are causing me harm in my relationship with You and not just put a patch over the problem. Make me a blessing to others. In the name of Jesus, amen.

DAY 2
INTIMACY WITH AN IMAGE

In the classic movie *The Shawshank Redemption*, the two main characters, Red and Andy, had a tense conversation near the end of the film, leaving Red with the fear that Andy was about to take his own life. Andy had just gotten out of solitary confinement and was daydreaming about getting out of prison. Red felt that those types of thoughts were harmful to Andy. Then Andy uttered the famous quote, "I guess it comes down to a simple choice, really. Get busy living, or get busy dying." Red was afraid that Andy had lost his hope. Hopelessness is a terrible thing because it means you have given up on the future. You've thrown in the towel. Far too many of us today are living in hopelessness.

You see this hopelessness when men walk away from their responsibilities. For adults, it might be to their families, to their communities, or their church. For you, it might be your school work, your team, your chores, or even your hobbies. You see this hopelessness when we no longer believe that God can make a difference in our lives. This hopelessness shows itself in a culture rife with conflict and depression. You may wonder, "Why?" Why did God allow this to get this bad? Sometimes, God allows things to get so low that the only way out is to look up.

In Ezekiel, we see God's judgment poured out on a culture filled with impurity and idol worship.

Read the Scripture below and answer the following questions.

The word of the Lord came to me: "Son of man, while the house of Israel
lived in their land, they defiled it with their conduct and actions . . .
So I poured out my wrath on them because of the blood they had shed
on the land, and because they had defiled it with their idols."
Ezekiel 36:16-17a, 18 (CSB)

In what ways is God's judgment evident in our world today?

Why is God's discipline actually good for us?

In Ezekiel's day and in our own, the world is filled with idols. Simply explained, idolatry is intimacy with an image. It's not necessarily bowing down to a carved statue stuck on a pole. An idol is anything that takes God's rightful rule in your life. Idols come in all shapes and sizes. Idolatry centers on alignment—you align your thoughts, words, and actions under what you value most.

What are some modern-day idols in our culture?

Making this more personal, what is an idol you struggle to place in its proper position under God?

What steps do you need to take to remove this idol and realign your life under God's rule?

Idolatry manifests itself in lifestyle choices that are contrary to God's expressed will in His Word. Consider what Paul said in his letter to the church at Colossae.

> *Therefore consider the members of your earthly body as dead to immorality,*
> *impurity, passion, evil desire, and greed, which amounts to idolatry.*
> Colossians 3:5

What are some ways idolatry becomes evident in the choices we make?
In what ways does greed reveal itself as idolatry in a person's life?

How should knowing that greed and impurity are considered idols by God affect the way you approach both?

Clinging to idols is forsaking the faithfulness of God. When the pendulum of our hearts swings toward idolatry, it slides away from God's love and power. However, the opposite is also true. When we forsake idols, our hearts swing into alignment with God's grace, faithfulness, power, and love in our lives. To embrace God's will and activate the flow of His love and power into our lives, we must turn away from idols. God has made it clear through His Word how to activate the flow of His love and power into your life, as well as how to deactivate it.

Turning away from common cultural temptations like impurity, evil desires, greed, pride, and selfishness enables you to open up the floodgate of God's love, favor, and blessing in your life. Idolatry is the number one factor in most of life's difficulties and disasters. Until we identify the root of idolatry and deal with it by removing it from our hearts, we cannot expect a different outcome.

Read Ezekiel 37:14. What power has God given to help you uncover and remove idols?

Describe a time when God removed a sinful pattern from your life or in someone's life whom you know. What did it take to root out the idols?

God has given us the means and the method for removing the idols that grip our hearts. He has given us new life in the Spirit, which provides the means to diagnose and dismiss our idols.

When God speaks of the resurrection in the Book of Ezekiel, it ultimately points us to Christ, who has conquered sin, death, and the grave. Through Jesus, we have been given the power of the Holy Spirit, and His life inside of us helps us put to death the idols our flesh leads us to pursue. Prayer and self-evaluation provide the methods for us to begin uprooting idols and casting them aside.

Describe what it means to "put to death" that which belongs to your earthly nature.

Read Psalm 139:23-24. Why is it essential for us to pause and take inventory of our hearts and lives regularly?

How does prayer contribute to spiritual growth?

Prayer lets us communicate directly with God. As we bring our requests, God begins to direct the thoughts and intentions of our hearts. We hear from Him and invite Him to put to death what is earthly in us. Let's end our time today by taking advantage of God's means and method for dealing with idolatry. And go watch *The Shawshank Redemption* (an edited version) to see what happened to Andy. You won't be disappointed.

Pray about one area in your life that needs to be "put to death" in order that it can be raised again according to God's Word and by His power. Ask God to draw your attention to what this is and how you can honor Him by letting it go and ridding its hold on your heart. Then, seek God's wisdom on what you can do to replace that gap in your life in a healthy, loving, and productive way.

DAY 3
A KEY WITHOUT A CAR

Imagine for a moment that someone handed you the keys to a brand new Lamborghini. The keys were all yours, they said. But the car was nowhere to be found. In fact, when you asked where the car was, all you were told is, "Somewhere." Fast forward a few weeks and, despite looking for the car for days on end, you still have not found it. At that point in time, how valuable are those keys?

Most people would answer that question, "Not very valuable at all." This is because keys—on their own—won't do you any good. Keys need to be coupled with a car for someone to understand their true value.

Similarly, most of us have access to Bibles, whether it's a physical copy or an app on your phone. But in order to unlock the true value of God's Word, we must commit to reading and applying it. Both pieces are necessary. God's Word must be understood and applied in order for it to activate God's power in your life.

Why is it spiritually dangerous to read God's Word without applying it to your life?

God's Word does not work just because you get excited about it when you read it. It doesn't work just because you heard a sermon or a podcast and got all fired up. It doesn't even work because you spent some time thinking about it or posted a verse on social media. It doesn't work because you could ace a Bible trivia contest. All of those things are nice. But if it's not applied, you won't get to experience the fullness of what God's Word is meant to do. To listen to God's Word but refuse to act on it causes us to do little more than waste our lives.

Often when God does spectacular things in the Bible, He asks His people to first take a step of obedience. Read the following verses and describe the common theme throughout.

As for you, lift up your staff, stretch out your hand over the sea, and divide it so that the Israelites can go through the sea on dry ground.
Exodus 14:16 (CSB)

It shall come about when the soles of the feet of the priests who carry the ark of the LORD, the Lord of all the earth, rest in the waters of the Jordan, the waters of the Jordan will be cut off, and the waters which are flowing down from above will stand in one heap.
Joshua 3:13

Before Lazarus was raised from the dead Jesus said:

"Remove the stone."
John 11:39a

List the simple steps of faith that preceded God's miraculous work in the verses you just read.

Why do you think God often uses our obedience to bring about the power of His Word in our lives?

Without faith, obedience, and application, hearing God's Word is just knowledge acquisition. Simply hearing the Word then moving on with life as if nothing has changed will never produce the supernatural intervention of God in your circumstances. Hearing, believing, and doing the Word of God is the foundation of wisdom from God.

Wisdom is both the ability and the responsibility of applying God's truth to life's choices. You can only identify a wise man or a fool by his decisions. We feel like dry bones wasting away because we haven't sought God's wisdom to bring about a different result. Godly wisdom sets men on a path out of the valley of sin.

Read the teaching of James on wisdom.

This wisdom is not that which comes down from above, but is earthly, natural, demonic. For where jealousy and selfish ambition exist, there is disorder and every evil thing. But the wisdom from above is first pure, then peaceable, gentle, reasonable, full of mercy and good fruits, unwavering, without hypocrisy. And the seed whose fruit is righteousness is sown in peace by those who make peace.

James 3:15-18

In what ways can you develop and strengthen your ability to apply godly wisdom to your everyday decisions?

Have you ever experienced a time where you tried to mix human thoughts with God's wisdom? What was the result?

God created you for more than you can ever imagine. But often we miss out on all that God can or will do through us because we pursue the wisdom of the world rather than the wisdom of God. Looking back to our opening illustration, we're the man standing in an empty garage holding the keys but not knowing what to do with them.

To embrace all that God has for you, you have to interact with His Word and His Spirit so that His Spirit can bring the wisdom of His Word to your heart and mind. That means more than just reading and knowing the Bible. You have to act on what it says (see Jas. 2:26). The power of God's promises remains dormant in your life unless activated by your faith.

Pursuing godly wisdom brings "good fruit." In other words, godly wisdom produces results. Embracing wisdom means we are obeying and applying God's truth to our lives. God is waiting on you to take your rightful place in this world. He is waiting for you to rise to the occasion and secure your spot of significance in His kingdom displayed here on earth. But that happens when you step out—fully, faithfully, and single-mindedly—according to the direction of His will.

In what way does God want to you to apply His Word in a more proactive way to the choices you have in your life today?

Where is God calling on you to seek His wisdom? In what area of life do you need a deeper understanding of His Word?

God is not going to force His wisdom on you. You have to discern it and then apply it. He has given each of us the free will to make our own choices, for good or for bad. But He has also given us the ability to ask Him for wisdom on how to make the best possible choices in whatever situation we face (see Jas. 1:5).

Pray for God's wisdom on how to know His Word better, understand it more fully, and apply it more diligently in your life. Ask Him to reveal to you those areas in the past where you have gotten off track from applying His truth to your choices. Once these are revealed, ask for His forgiveness and guidance on how to restore what has been broken or damaged due to those decisions. Then seek to obey Him in what He reveals to you to do. He can revive anything in your life that seems beyond redemption. But remember, it requires your participation in the process.

But Peter said, "I do not possess silver and gold, but what I do have I give to you: In the name of Jesus Christ the Nazarene—walk!" And seizing him by the right hand, he raised him up; and immediately his feet and his ankles were strengthened.

ACTS 3:6-7

WEEK 3
GET UP

KINGDOM MEN RISING

START

Welcome to group session 3 of *Kingdom Men Rising*.

Last session, we considered how God's Word brings purpose and direction to our lives. We saw how God can take a weak or distracted spiritual life and make it alive again like Ezekiel saw in the valley of dry bones.

Describe one meaningful truth from last session with the group.

This week, we're going to be talking about how to get up and overcome what is holding us back. As an illustration, have guys in your group that are approximately the same height and size pair up and sit on the ground. First, ask them to sit with their backs against a wall and stand up individually without using their hands. They'll be able to do it (because they are young men), but it won't be as easy as if they used their hands or had help from their partner. Then have them sit back to back and lock arms, then try to stand up. It will be surprisingly quick and easy for them to stand as long as they are matched correctly with height and size. This is a picture of how we as men can be there for each other. Back to back, arms locked, going through life together, and helping each other stand up under the pressures of this world.

What are some ways are we able to help each other get up after we have been knocked down?

Sometimes life's difficulties knock us out, beat us down, or get us off the field completely. But there are other times when a helpful friend can go a long way in getting us back on our feet and in the game again. Standing up after you've been knocked down is rarely a solo experience. It takes others coming alongside you to lift you, encourage you, and strengthen you until you can once again stand and be in a place to help others stand as well.

Ask someone to pray before watching the video teaching.

Get Up
WATCH

Use this space to take notes during the video teaching.

MAN UP

Use the following questions to discuss the video teaching.

Read Acts 3:1-2 together.

Now Peter and John were going up to the temple at the ninth hour, the hour of prayer. And a man who had been lame from his mother's womb was being carried along, whom they used to set down every day at the gate of the temple which is called Beautiful, in order to beg alms of those who were entering the temple.

Acts 3:1-2

This man sat down every day at a place called "Beautiful," but his life was anything but beautiful. He had been crippled all his life and had to be carried to a place to beg.

What kind of hardship do you imagine this man dealt with day after day?

Why does suffering—physical or otherwise—often impact our spiritual lives?

Many of the things that cripple us in our own lives come about through comparison. Comparing yourself to others can have a debilitating effect on what you do. If you ever see two quarterbacks competing for the same role, they will often underperform. This is because they know they are being scrutinized and compared. Yet when a franchise shows confidence in one quarterback and assures him of his role, he will regularly play with a higher level of competence.

Describe some of the ways we limit our own potential by comparing ourselves to other people.

How does comparison often lead to emotional pain and hardship?

Lameness comes in all shapes and sizes. We can be lame spiritually, where we're so far from God that we lean into our own understanding. We can be lame emotionally, not asking for the help we need to help us get healthy. We can be lame morally, not making the right choices, abusing others, and also abusing ourselves. We can be lame relationally because we're hanging out with the wrong people and doing the wrong things. And we fake it; we pretend that we can stand up and man up. We use all the right words but can't stand on our own two feet. And that makes us like this man in Acts 3—a "spiritual beggar."

What does it look like to be a "spiritual beggar"?

We all enter the kingdom of heaven poor in spirit (see Matt. 5:3). At some point, we have to get up from the ground, get healed, and get help. Then we can help other spiritual beggars rise up to be the people God created them to be. Once the lame man was healed, he got up and started praising God (see Acts 3:8). The power of God became active in his life, and he returned the praise to God.

What specific, practical steps can you take this week to overcome any personal spiritual lameness in your life?

Now consider who needs your help. What specific, practical steps can you take this week to help someone else overcome any personal spiritual lameness in his life?

PRAYER

Father, You have charged us with the calling of rising as kingdom men. It is not okay to stay down, defeated, and bound by any emotional or spiritual strongholds. We ask that You shine a light onto those areas in our lives where we need to heal, grow, and become stronger. Give us the humility we need to ask others for help. Give us the wisdom we need to help others who can benefit from our help. In the name of Jesus, amen.

STAND TALL AND TELL OTHERS

Just like our bodies can experience muscle atrophy due to poor nutrition or a lack of use, our spiritual lives can deteriorate when we give up or throw in the towel due to difficulties we face. But God gives us four key principles, based on the story of the lame man, we can apply in order to overcome spiritual and emotional lameness. We find these in Acts 3:

> *And he began to give them his attention, expecting to receive something from them. But Peter said, "I do not possess silver and gold, but what I do have I give to you: In the name of Jesus Christ the Nazarene—walk!" And seizing him by the right hand, he raised him up; and immediately his feet and his ankles were strengthened. With a leap he stood upright and began to walk; and he entered the temple with them, walking and leaping and praising God.*
>
> **Acts 3:5-8**

1
GIVE GOD YOUR ATTENTION

The first step you must take in restoring spiritual strength when it has been lost is to turn your attention to God. Like the lame man begging at the temple, expect to receive something. What God gives you may be different from what you expect to get, but that doesn't rid you of your personal responsibility to look to Him with hope.

2
RECEIVE HIS HELP

God's help can come to you in any number of ways. It may come through a friend, a parent, a book, a sermon, a small group, a coach, or a pastor or mentor. However God chooses to send you the guidance and wisdom you need on the path to your spiritual restoration, it is up to you to receive it. No one is going to do it all for you. Participate in the process of your own healing.

3 STAND UP

Once God gives you what you need in order to be lifted from the slump of spiritual lameness, be willing to stand up and take your next step. Do not fail to realize that God has healed you and strengthened you to stand. Don't sit back down. Muscles develop as you use them, so keep going. The same is true for your spiritual and emotional life. You may only go so far at the start, but with time, you will increase your distance.

PRAISE GOD AND 4 TELL OTHERS

As God continues to strengthen you and rebuild the parts of your life that were broken, do not keep it to yourself. Show others what He has done in your life. Demonstrate to others what is possible. In this way, you encourage others in their own healing as well. As you praise God and tell of His power, you create a ripple effect of personal growth in others, too.

Which of the principles do you need to embrace right now?

What is a step you can take right now to embrace this principle?

Father, help me to give You my full attention and be willing to receive the help You are offering me right now. Give me the strength to stand up and walk with You. As I grow stronger in You, help me to always give You the praise and tell others about what You have done for me. In the name of Jesus, amen.

DAY 2
PARTICIPATE IN THE PROCESS

Have you ever gotten a card for your birthday, opened the envelope, pulled the card out and didn't even read it, but just went straight to looking at what's inside of it? You did this because you wanted to know if the person who sent you the card had given you any money. Or, maybe, if it was from your grandparents, if you got a check. If you were to be honest, you would admit that you don't even care that much about the card. You only care about what's inside the card!

This was the attitude of the lame man at the Beautiful gate. He wanted the money. He had no concept or even hope of being healed. Why? Because he had been brought there day after day to beg, and never once did someone offer to help his physical condition. He waited and waited, hoping for money, but Peter and John had something so much greater.

Sometimes, waiting like this lame man is good for us. God has a way of delaying His provision and intervention in our lives for a greater purpose. One of the purposes is to be sure He has our full attention first.

Read Psalm 62:1 and Psalm 69:3 then answer the following questions.

My soul waits in silence for God only;
From Him is my salvation.
Psalm 62:1

I am weary with my crying; my throat is parched;
My eyes fail while I wait for my God.
Psalm 69:3

Describe a time when God didn't give you what you wanted, but came through at a later date. What did the waiting teach you about God? About yourself?

The lame man from Acts 3 was taken to the gate of the temple every day (see v. 2). Even though this was an area with heavy foot traffic, he was likely ignored. As Peter and John walked by the lame man, Peter said, "Look at us!" (v. 4). Now, if Peter had to say that, that means the man wasn't looking at them to begin with. That gives us great insight into this lame man. Peter needed this man's undivided attention. He needed him to focus. If this man truly wanted a solution, he'd need to pay close attention to Peter right then. He needed to be part of the solution.

Healing and empowerment are not a one-way gift through the touch of a magic wand. True healing requires your desire, responsibility, and focus. That's why Jesus would often ask the question, "Do you want to be made well?" He didn't just walk around tapping people on the head, giving health and healing to whoever was near. Keep in mind, crowds of people flocked around Jesus wherever He went. Lines formed. Inevitably, people walked away unhealed. Rather, Jesus would ask if the person was willing to be made whole. Healing and wholeness come in a process of belief and through a desire to be made well.

How does our personal participation in the process of healing lead to deeper growth?

How does our participation help us understand those seasons where God asks or expects us to wait on His timing?

Physical therapists can do wonders with patients who want to be made well. But if a patient does not have the will to get better, the improvements are typically less drastic, if there are any at all. Oftentimes, a physical therapist will note on a patient's chart that the patient is either "noncompliant" or "noncooperative." This lets the other nurses or therapists gain insight into why the progression toward wholeness is moving so slowly. When God restores the parts of us that have been damaged by sin or wounded through personal neglect or harm, He wants our cooperation in the process. Without it, long-term progress does not take place.

In what ways can a person cooperate with God in the process of healing from spiritual lameness or emotional wounds?

Just like it is unwise for a man to lift a large amount of weights alone in a gym without a spotter or someone to encourage and help, growth in the spiritual life does not happen in a silo. We are all part of a collective process, cooperating with God and others in our healing and spiritual development. Our willingness to experience life more closely with others and more humbly before God will have a large impact on how much lameness we are able to overcome, both individually and as a group. We cannot be content with past victories; we must continue to participate in our faith journey as Paul wrote in Philippians 2.

> *So then, my beloved, just as you have always obeyed, not as in my presence only,*
> *but now much more in my absence, work out your salvation with fear and trembling*
> *for it is God who is at work in you, both to will and to work for His good pleasure.*
> **Philippians 2:12-13**

On a scale of 1-10, how much effort do you put into your own spiritual healing and growth?

1   2   3   4   5   6   7   8   9   10

What makes it difficult for you to invest more than you do?

On a scale of 1-10, how much effort does God put into your spiritual healing and growth, both to will and to work for His good pleasure?

1   2   3   4   5   6   7   8   9   10

How can you reveal your willingness to cooperate with God on a greater level so that He can develop and unleash you to do His kingdom work?

What practical steps can you take to participate more intentionally in your own personal path to spiritual maturity, strength, healing, and growth?

Who is a more mature kingdom man who can help you get up from the ground when you're down and in need of spiritual strength and healing?

Pray about your willingness to participate in the process of healing, helping, and growing as a young kingdom man. Ask God to reveal where you have been unwilling to either lend a hand or receive a hand toward greater spiritual maturity. Seek ways you can become better connected with other guys so that iron can truly sharpen iron as Scripture says it should (see Prov. 27:17).

DAY 3
DO YOU KNOW WHAT YOU KNOW?

A POW is a prisoner of war—a person who has been captured by the enemy and is held hostage during conflict. The opposing forces control the prisoner's living conditions, activities, and movements. Many of us live like POWs, but rather than being prisoners of war, we're prisoners of addictive behavior. We have been captured by the enemy, and there appears to be no way of escape. We feel trapped in situations and circumstances that the world labels as addiction. Drugs, sex, pornography, alcohol, bad relationships, negative self-talk, food, phones, activity, comfort—these things become coping mechanisms for life's pain, disappointments, and boredom. When an action or activity begins to influence you more than you influence it, it can leave you feeling trapped.

Addictive behavior is like quicksand. The harder you try to get out of a situation, the deeper you sink. Human methods can never set you free from a spiritual stranglehold on your life. Rather, these attempts will make you sink faster.

Another problem that arises when someone is sinking in quicksand involves focus. Remember when Peter stepped off the boat to walk to Jesus on the waves (see Matt. 14:28-31)? Things were going great, then his vision shifted and his circumstances overtook his focus on Christ. Where you look matters. If a person stares only at the sand surrounding him, he will miss the stick being held out to him that he must grasp to be dragged out. We rely on human methods when only spiritual methods can deliver.

Consider Paul's words about the conflict going on all around us.

> *For although we live in the flesh, we do not wage war according to the flesh, since the weapons of our warfare are not of the flesh, but are powerful through God for the demolition of strongholds. We demolish arguments and every proud thing that is raised up against the knowledge of God, and we take every thought captive to obey Christ.*
>
> **2 Corinthians 10:3-5 (CSB)**

What does it mean when Paul wrote, "...although we live in the flesh, we do not wage war according to the flesh" (v.3)?

What must happen first in order for us to overcome a stronghold in our life?

Strongholds are places where the enemy has a grip on your life and won't easily let you go. One reason strongholds are so powerful is that they're so entrenched. They become entrenched when we buy into the lie that our situation is hopeless. Satan's goal is to get you to believe that, by nature, you are addicted to porn, that you are a manipulative or a negative person, that you are controlled by fear or shame, that nothing will ever change. Once you adopt this line of thinking, these unhelpful patterns become entrenched fortresses that are difficult to remove. As a result, your behavior deteriorates even more because we have a tendency to act according to who we believe we are.

The only solution is to tear down these strongholds by "taking every thought captive to the obedience of Christ" (v. 5). This means replacing your harmful and untrue thoughts with the better promises of God. Embracing this advice from Scripture reprograms your mind and releases you from spiritual strongholds. You become free yourself so you can then help others rise to do the same.

Name some common cultural influences that can be used by the enemy to keep your mind hearing, rehearsing, and believing the lies of this world.

What thoughts do you need to take captive?

Overcoming personal strongholds is a two-part process of reprogramming your mind. First, identify God's thoughts on a matter, and secondly, align your own thinking under the rule of His truth. The truth, then, will set you free (see John 8:32). Let's work through this process together.

Write down a struggle you have, then answer the following questions:

Write out your thoughts on this struggle. Be specific.

What promises of Christ speak to this struggle? Get your Bible or Bible app and find specific Scriptures that speak to your struggle.

Identify the ways your thinking is out of alignment with Christ's thoughts.

How must you adjust your thoughts to align under the rule of Christ's truth?

Keep in mind that just acknowledging the truth won't break any bonds. John 8:32 says that you "will know" the truth and then be set free. The word for "will know" in the original Greek of the New Testament refers not just to head knowledge, but deep and personal familiarity with a subject. To know the truth, in the biblical form of this word, is to make it an essential part of who you are. It is to know and be known by it, in the deepest, most authentic place in you. To know ourselves in this way, we need to consistently be in God's Word.

For the word of God is living and active and sharper than any two-edged sword, and piercing as far as the division of soul and spirit, of both joints and marrow, and able to judge the thoughts and intentions of the heart.

Hebrews 4:12

Describe the difference between "knowing" something in your mind and "knowing" something personally. Why is this important when it comes to knowing God's Word?

How has God's Word freed you from hardship and sin in the past?

As you seek to heal from any and every spiritual and emotional stronghold you may face, or as you seek to guide others into healing as well, be sure to identify what Jesus says on the matter, and then memorize it, meditate on it, and apply it. It is not enough to simply be aware of the truth, just like it is not enough to simply be aware of your dinner. You must eat your dinner for it to have any positive impact on your body. Similarly, you must consume the Word of God in such a way that it becomes an essential part of your nature on a regular basis.

Pray for God to inspire you to know His Word on a deeper level. Invite Him to show you ways you can discover truth in His Word beyond what you have done in the past. Ask Him to connect you with others who have a similar hunger for His Word. In this way, you can grow together and strengthen each other as you rise together as kingdom men.

The angel of the LORD appeared to him and said to him, "The LORD is with you, O valiant warrior."

JUDGES 6:12

WEEK 4
GET GOING

START

Welcome to session 4 of *Kingdom Men Rising.*

Look back at your answers to the exercise on pages 53-54. Would someone share what they learned from this experience?

Last session, we learned about getting up from our struggles. This week, we'll talk about how to get going to move beyond the idols in our lives. As an illustration, before your group meets, snap a picture of your wedding photo with your phone or bring one to the group meeting. If you are not married, find a photo of a family member's wedding or someone else in your life who has demonstrated faithfulness in their marriage. Talk about the vows that are taken at a wedding and how silly it would be if a couple getting married decided to only be married on days that start with T's and S's, and on every other day they could consider themselves unmarried.

How do loyalty and commitment contribute to healthy relationships?

No man entering a marriage relationship intends to cheat on his spouse. Likewise, no man in a marriage relationship desires for his wife to cheat on him. Faithfulness is foundational to a marriage. Somehow, we don't always connect this idea when it comes to maintaining and cultivating our relationship with God. To cheat on God is to set any competing interest in our hearts at the same level as Him. That could show up in a number of areas—entertainment, focus, relationships, hobbies, addictions, money, and many other things.

As we've already seen in this study, idolatry is intimacy with an image. We don't have to bow down to a carved statue to be idolaters. We worship idols when we allow anything to take God's rightful place in our lives.

Ask someone to pray before watching the video teaching.

WATCH

Use this space to take notes during the video teaching.

MAN UP

Use the following questions to discuss the video teaching.

Read Jonah 2:8 together.

Those who cling to worthless idols turn away from God's love for them.
Jonah 2:8 (NIV)

What does it mean to "cling" to an idol? How do idols cause us to "turn away from God's love" for us?

From Genesis to Revelation, you will see God condemning idols. An idol is a "God substitute" or any person, place, thing, or thought that you look to over Him. There are primitive idols—like golden calfs—that we may not identify with today. But then there are American idols, which are the things we struggle with the most in our country. It can be materialism. It can be greed. It can be relationships. It can be sports. It can be comfort. It can be anything that has come before God in your heart. And God will always judge idolatry.

We just listed five idols that plague us as guys. How can each of these things become idols that rob our affection for God?

Materialism:

Greed:

Relationships:

Sports:

Comfort:

How are the idols we just listed widely accepted by guys today?

How can a sense of entitlement lead to idolatry?

As we read in Jonah 2:8, living with idols creates distance in our relationship with God. Like a man cheating on his wife, our attention is divided between God and the idols we are pursuing. Far too many of us are failing to advance in our lives as God desires or to thrive in our schools and communities as we have been designed to do because we have chosen to embrace idolatry in one form or another. Many pursue idols without even realizing what they're doing.

What do you think has contributed to a lack of awareness of how our personal choices lead us to idolatry?

Too many of us today have identified with too many false gods. We need to step up, get going, and move away from the lifeless idols robbing us of spiritual vitality and impact. When we put away our idols and embrace God's better plan for our lives, He will use us to do something bigger than what we could have ever done on our own.

Gideon and Moses are examples of men God used beyond their limited human ability. How did God use these men? How did God overcome their limitations?

Describe a time in your life or in the life of someone you know when God's purpose or calling was bigger than what could be done alone.

PRAYER

Father, remove from my heart any dependence or loyalty on anything I place higher than You. I confess any and all idolatry I have allowed in my life and I take full responsibility for having let it into my heart. Forgive me and show me a better way. Give me a "burning bush" experience and an encounter with You in order to guide me in a new direction of honoring You first and foremost in all I think, say, and do. In the name of Jesus, amen.

GOD GOES FIRST

Gideon was a man of no reputation. He would not have been the first chosen in any backyard football game. And where Gideon lacked in known abilities, he equaled in a lack of confidence. Yet God used Gideon in a mighty way in order to defeat a more powerful army who had held His people oppressed for far too long. How did Gideon rise up and become victorious? He learned that spiritual success in spiritual war depends entirely upon spiritual solutions.

Gideon first had to learn that God was His source. When we meet Gideon, he was fearful and timid. But God had other plans, as He often does. Gideon had to learn to see himself from God's viewpoint. In your own Bible or Bible app, read Judges 6:11-16. These verses describe Gideon's call from God. After you read the story, consider these three principles we can learn from this account.

GOD SEES OUR CIRCUMSTANCES CLEARLY

Gideon was overwhelmed with his circumstances because he failed to see that God was with him (vv. 11-13). The Midianites were fearsome enemies, but they were no match for God. As He brought Israel out of Egypt, He would deliver them from the Midianites. He was waiting on Gideon's participation.

GOD SEES A WARRIOR WHERE WE SEE A WIMP

God saw Gideon differently than Gideon saw himself. When God charged Gideon with a task, Gideon responded, "my family is the least in Manasseh, and I am the youngest in my father's house" (v. 15). While he thought he was a wimp, God knew he was a "valiant warrior" (v. 12). Gideon was so overwhelmed by his circumstances that he forgot how God saw him.

3

GOD SEES HIS OWN ABILITY MORE THAN OUR LIMITATIONS

God told Gideon He was with him and that Gideon was a warrior (see v. 12). Based on that truth, God sent Gideon on a mission—He told Gideon he would "defeat Midian as one man" (v. 16). Gideon only saw his ability instead of God's. For too long, he had trusted in idols rather than the God of Israel, but God was about to change all of that.

Rising up as a kingdom man requires alignment with God's plans and purposes. As we see from the life of Gideon, God's presence produces the victory we seek. Yet one way we often remove God's presence from our lives is through the sin of idolatry. Gideon had to first tear down the idols in order to open the gap for God to move in his situation (see Judg. 6:25-32).

Which of these principles is most meaningful to you?

Which do you need to take hold of right now?

Father, help me know that You see my circumstances far more clearly than I do. Help me to believe that Your Spirit inside of me makes me a warrior and not a wimp. Help me to trust that Your ability is greater than any limitation I may have or perceive in myself. Thank You for desiring to use me. Help me to follow You where You lead. In the name of Jesus, amen.

DAY 2
USE WHAT HE GAVE YOU

We should not expect God to do something through us if we are not first willing to get things right within us. Think about it like a domino effect:

> A messed-up man contributes to a messed-up family, which then contributes to a messed-up church. A messed-up church contributes to a messed-up community, which then contributes to a messed-up state, which then contributes to a messed-up country. And a messed-up country contributes to a messed-up world. Therefore, if you want a better world comprised of better countries made up of better states containing better communities housing better churches attended by better families, it starts off with being a better man. It starts with you. Right here. Right now.

The deliverance of the entire nation of Israel from the hands of the Midianites started with one man seeking a better world. It started with Gideon, right in his own home. Before Gideon could ever take on a national enemy, he had to first tear down his idols. God had raised up Gideon for a mighty conquest, but he had to demonstrate faithfulness first. Before God would bless Gideon's work, He asked him to be obedient with what he had around him.

Read Matthew 13:12 and Luke 16:10 and answer the following questions.

> *For whoever has, to him more shall be given, and he will have an abundance;*
> *but whoever does not have, even what he has shall be taken away from him.*
> **Matthew 13:12**

> *He who is faithful in a very little thing is faithful also in much; and he*
> *who is unrighteous in a very little thing is unrighteous also in much.*
> **Luke 16:10**

Restate the teaching of Jesus in those two verses in your own words.

Why is it important to demonstrate faithfulness with what you have?

What are some reasons we might not be willing to use what God has given us?

Why might a person wait on God to give him more or to open doors rather than moving forward with what he has right now?

Describe the end result of not investing your spiritual gifts in those around you. How does this contribute to the continuation of a chaotic culture?

Faithfulness with what you have right now and right where you are is always the first step toward further use in God's kingdom. We see this not only with Gideon, but throughout the Bible and in our own lives. We expect God to move in our lives, but we refuse to get going. Instead, we stand still in place, waiting for the right time, when God has given us everything we need all along.

God wants you to follow Him right where you are. He wants you to be faithful now—whether it's with your relationships and friends or even in your school, neighborhood, and church. Don't waste your time on visions of great future things if you are not willing to get moving where God has placed you now. Waiting on "the right time" can be an idol just like anything else.

List some of the benefits you receive when you choose to let go of your plans and trust solely in God and His plan.

Despite having all of these benefits, why do you think some of us still choose to "play it safe" and not risk full surrender to God's will and ways?

What might it look like for you to overcome the idol of comfort?

We experience our greatest spiritual success when we are willing to lay down our plans, purposes, devices, and strategies and completely devote ourselves to God and His way. God is not interested in divided hearts. He wants your undivided attention, devotion, and obedience. He wants you to get up and get going toward the plan He has created for you to live out.

> *"For I know the plans that I have for you," declares the* LORD, *"plans for welfare and not for calamity to give you a future and a hope."*
> **Jeremiah 29:11**

Life is not found in sitting around and waiting on the right time. Neither is it found in looking for other people to stand up and make a difference. You are to use your voice, your actions, and your life to advance God's kingdom agenda on earth. If and when enough kingdom men choose to rise up for what is right and just in this world, the enemy will be forced to back down. But we can only rise up when we are first willing to let go of the plans and the idols that have locked us in place for far too long. God has given us all we need to get going. We need to take the steps He has laid before us.

Spend some time considering God's leading in your life to make a difference in your home, school, church, and in the activities you participate in. What do you believe God is asking you to do in order to advance His kingdom of love, righteousness, and justice here on earth?

God will often use our skills and knowledge from past experiences in order to enable us to make a greater impact for good in the lives of those around us.

What are some identifiable skills and talents God has developed in you which could be used to further His plans for well-being in your circles of influence?

What step can you take this week to break out of your comfort zone and seek to make a difference for God in an area you have never sought to before?

Pray about how you can rise up as a kingdom man in order to impact your home, school, church, community, and beyond. Ask God to reveal to you anything He has already equipped you with which can be used to bring about a positive impact on the lives of those around you. Ask Him for the wisdom and courage to go after the plan and purpose He has for you to fulfill.

DAY 3
STAND IN THE GAP

A quick but relevant question for you: do you know that you are somebody special? You're not ordinary; you are extraordinary. You're not average; you're of the highest quality. And because of this truth, God is calling you to do something bigger than you ever dreamed was possible.

But He needs you to stop hiding like Gideon and stop letting the culture hold you hostage. God desires for you to deal with the idols that are consuming you, as well as those that surround you. He wants you to publicly and unashamedly decide, "Yes, I'm going to be defined by God now. And I'm going to let it be known that I don't deal with idols. I surrender to and follow the true and living God."

Read Ezekiel 22:30 then answer the following questions.

I searched for a man among them who would build up the wall and stand in the gap before Me for the land, so that I would not destroy it; but I found no one.

Ezekiel 22:30

How can we "stand in the gap" before God?

What are some visible and clear actions we can take to stand up for righteousness and justice in order to advance God's kingdom agenda?

God can give you the ability to stand up for Him, but it will take courage. Gideon was so frightened that when God reached out to him, he was literally hiding. Yet by the end of the story of Gideon's life, he had risen to become a feared and honored man of great courage. In fact, he had so much courage that his reputation spread (see Judg. 6:32).

You have all you need within you to do and be the same. But it will take standing up for what you believe in and following God's leading in your life. You can't remain hidden, seeking to protect what is yours, and expect to defeat the enemy. You have a choice to make. Will you live as a man of fear and preservation or will you lead those within your circle of influence to spiritual victory as a kingdom man of courage?

What's the difference between "privately declaring" and "publicly proclaiming" your allegiance to God and standing for Him?

Why do you think so few of us are willing to rise up and publicly align ourselves with God in today's culture?

What are some strategies the enemy uses to keep us silent on what is right and true?

Many of us, like Gideon, are initially afraid to stand in the gap. We can't wait for an absence of fear in order to step out in faith. The time to be obedient as a kingdom man doesn't always come when it's calm. Sometimes that obedience takes place in a mixture of emotions. There is no doubt that Gideon was scared as he was traipsing around at night when he went to pull down his family's altars (see Judg. 6:27).

Courage does not require the absence of fear. Courage means right actions taken in spite of fear's presence. There's nothing courageous about doing something you know will succeed without any opposition. Courage occurs when you rise up to do the task that looks impossible.

When we commit to "get going," how can our action steps override our fear?

Describe how Satan uses "fear" to paralyze people from doing what is right.

When has God helped you or someone you know push past fears to make an impact? What was learned from that experience?

Kingdom men are living in our own sort of Midian today. We are sorely outnumbered. Our broader culture has not only abandoned God, but has taken up the offensive against the one true God. Much of what our society values stands against key doctrines and beliefs from Scripture. This is our reality, whether we like it or not. We can pretend it doesn't exist, but it does.

However, it doesn't take millions to take ground back for Jesus. In fact, as we saw in the story of Gideon, three hundred will do (see Judg. 7). Gideon demonstrated this truth as he led his charge in the dark night. Similarly, we are to rise up and get going to do what God has called each of us to do so that we might advance His kingdom agenda on earth. All we have to do is to get going and trust that God is on our side.

We must do this personally, and we must also do this collectively. If we sit around waiting for a majority, we will have waited too long. God knows how to handle the issues we face. It's our role to repent of our sins, trust God, and then do what He says. A few kingdom men in the hands of one mighty God can route any evil that opposes them.

Can you identify ways you may have been able to advance God's kingdom through something you said or did, but you chose not to out of fear?

What are some common fears that keep you from moving? List them below.

How can God be able to supply all you need despite your fears?

Where is God calling you to stand in the gap?

What is one step you can take this week to stand for God in this gap?

Pray right now and commit your life to living courageously as a kingdom man. Ask God to make it clear to you the level of impact you are to have for His kingdom, His glory, and others' good. Also, ask God as you pray that He will place men in your life who can lead you so that you will continue to grow as a young kingdom man. Then pray that God would place people in your life that you can build up and encourage as they grow into young kingdom men as well.

By this all men will know that you are
My disciples, if you have love for one another.

JOHN 13:35

WEEK 5
GET ALONG

START

Share one key takeaway from last session's group or personal studies.

Last week, we talked about how idols keep us stuck in place and stagnant in God's kingdom. This week, we will tackle barriers that keep us from working together for our shared kingdom agenda. As an illustration, have your guys pair up as best you can according to strength and arm wrestle each other. Tell them that they have a minute to arm wrestle and every time someone wins a match within that minute they'll get a quarter (be sure you bring a handful of quarters to the group meeting). Most likely, they'll instantly start trying to win as quickly as possible, working against each other. But if they are evenly matched, there won't be many victories in a minute's time. After the minute is up, hand out the quarters to the winners and then offer another perspective. Tell them that if they had worked together and just went back and forth taking turns winning, they could have probably made a few dollars they could share.

Why did it not occur to either of you to work together instead of competing against each other?

Why is working together and being unified in approach and purpose critical for life in the body of Christ?

True unity does not mean sameness in every aspect of life. It does not mean we are to all like the same things, listen to the same music, talk the same way, or eat the same food. True unity is about something much bigger. Unity is about oneness of purpose. *Unity matters.*

This principle especially applies to kingdom disciples following Christ. Much of the chaos and defeat we experience today is a result of division among each other. We need to unify under the goal of advancing God's kingdom agenda on earth. Even as young kingdom men, you can play a key role in healing the division in our culture by rising up, working together, and living in unity together as brothers in Christ.

Ask someone to pray before watching the video teaching.

Get Along

WATCH

Use this space to take notes during the video teaching.

MAN UP

Use the following questions to discuss the video teaching.

Read John 13:35 and John 17:20-21 together.

By this all men will know that you are My disciples, if you have love for one another.
John 13:35

I do not ask on behalf of these alone, but for those also who believe in Me through their word; that they may all be one; even as You, Father, are in Me and I in You, that they also may be in Us, so that the world may believe that You sent Me.
John 17:20-21

Why do you think demonstrating "love for one another" reveals to others that we are Christ's kingdom disciples?

Jesus prayed the verses in John 17 right before He was arrested and put on trial. Why would unity have been so important to Jesus in His final moments before His crucifixon?

In a world of chaos and confusion, of disconnectedness and disunity, we're needing kingdom men to rise up and bring harmony where there's conflict and peace where there is chaos. Now is the time to get along. We bear a unique responsibility to set the stage for a comeback and healing in our lives and in our land. One of the things we must begin to grasp at a greater level is that God is a God of unity and togetherness. God does not hang out in atmospheres of division. He cannot. It goes against the nature of His being and essence.

Describe some ways we can "rise up and bring harmony" in the area of division and disunity in our world.

Ephesians 4:3 urges Christians to be "diligent to preserve the unity of the Spirit in the bond of peace." What does it means to "preserve" unity as opposed to "create" it?

Why do you think it is our role as believers to "preserve" unity?

In cooking and baking, eggs often act as an ingredient that brings two other ingredients together. God has called His people to become like eggs in the culture. We are to bring people together. We do this based on God's standard, not based on how we were raised, the neighborhood we live in, the school we go to, the color of our skin, or the class that we are. Before and beyond all those designations, we are primarily followers of Christ.

What are some of the challenges we may face or have faced in seeking to be unifiers in our world?

God has a standard. It's a high standard that involves living in love and unity. He is calling each of us—as much as it depends on us—to live at peace with everyone (see Rom. 12:18). Unity requires intentional effort and calls us out of our comfort zone. But God never said that living as a kingdom man was easy. Nothing worthwhile comes easy. But it will be worth it as we impact our broken and chaotic world with the healing balm of oneness.

Share one practical action you can put in place this week to intentionally preserve unity where disunity has taken hold. Make it personal. It could be something you do at school, home, on social media, or in your church and community.

PRAYER

Father, in a world that consistently promotes disunity, division, distrust, anger, and blame—help us to be young kingdom men who honor and reflect You through all we say and do. Grant us the wisdom and courage necessary to stand strong together. Bring unity where there is division and help us to be people of peace who accomplish much for your kingdom. In the name of Jesus, amen.

IDENTIFYING YOUR IDENTITY

When an athlete wins a gold medal in the Olympic games, they do not ask the winner what his or her favorite song is and play it. No, the song that plays is the national anthem of the country he or she represents. This is because his or her identity with his or her nation supersedes all else at that point in time.

Unfortunately, far too many Christians allow other things to define them rather than Jesus, the One who died for them and lives in them. Because of this, we have identity confusion breeding division everywhere. Galatians 2:20 is one of the greatest verses in the Bible about unity.

Read this verse and examine the following principles taken from it:

I have been crucified with Christ; and it is no longer I who live, but Christ lives in me; and the life which I now live in the flesh I live by faith in the Son of God, who loved me and gave Himself up for me.

Galatians 2:20

Here are three principles we can gain from this verse to help us live in unity:

1
DEFINE YOUR HUMANITY BY YOUR CHRISTIANITY.

In English, the job of the adjective is to describe the noun. As a young kingdom man, Christian is to be the adjective that defines you—not your race, creed, culture, background, or preferences. Whenever these things conflict with the living God as the definer of who you are, you must adjust and align yourself once again under Him.

2
LAY DOWN YOUR OWN DESIRES.

Make God's standards and His rules your overarching desires. When Paul wrote that "it is no longer I who live," he was stating that Christ now lives in him. Similarly, Christ now lives in each of us. We are His servants and we are to honor Him by living according to His desires, not our own.

3
LIVE BY FAITH IN THE SON OF GOD.

Find friends who will hold you accountable to living a life of faith according to God's standards and His rule of love. Take time to assess your relationships. If there is consistent disunity in any of them, seek to address it. Surround yourself with like-minded people who will seek to preserve the unity of the Spirit in the bond of Christ.

Which of these principles do you need to take hold of most today?

Father, I want to be defined by You. Help me to lay down my desires and pick up what you want for me because I know that you love me. Help me to live by faith and surround myself with people who do the same. In the name of Jesus, amen.

DAY 2
GOD DID IT

When things go wrong in your life, where do you look first? Do you try and find how you may have contributed to what went wrong, or are you quick to blame someone or something else?

Oftentimes it feels easier to blame something outside of ourselves when we go through troubles in life. But there is someone we rarely think to blame who may actually be behind the issues we are facing. God Himself. To be clear, God is never responsible for evil or suffering. He cannot sin or cause sin; it is against His holy nature. However, God will often allow us to sit in the disorder of our lives in order that we might return to Him and experience refreshing and revival.

God doesn't stir up issues for us to deal with just for the fun of it. But He does allow negative consequences in our lives to crop up when He is trying to get our attention. Rather than pointing fingers at everyone else when difficulties arise, we might want to take a moment to focus on the One who is really in charge. When we do, we will find that the way to solve life's challenging situations is sometimes easier than we had once thought.

In the history of Israel and Judah, Asa was one of the better kings, particularly during the first part of his reign. In 2 Chronicles 15, the Spirit of God came upon the prophet Azariah to encourage Asa in his religious reforms and remind him what happens when people forsake God.

Read 2 Chronicles 15:3-6 and answer the following questions.

For many years Israel has been without the true God, without a teaching priest, and without instruction, but when they turned to the Lord God of Israel in their distress and sought him, he was found by them. In those times there was no peace for those who went about their daily activities because the residents of the lands had many conflicts. Nation was crushed by nation and city by city, for God troubled them with every possible distress.

2 Chronicles 15:3-6 (CSB)

Why would God trouble people "with every possible distress"?

Do you believe that God still "troubles" people today? Can you think of any examples that you feel may be from God's hand?

Can you identify a time in your life when you can see God allowed troubles in order to draw you back to Him and His rule over you?

Like the Israelites, in what ways does our distress have a way of making us turn back to God?

When this Bible study was originally written, our nation and world were in the middle of the Covid-19 pandemic. But we were actually facing multiple pandemics: a medical pandemic and a cultural pandemic. Yet deeper still and at the root of both of these sat a spiritual pandemic.

Observing what took place during the onset of this unusual time, it wasn't hard to notice that we had wandered far from the value system established by God for how human beings are to live, act, and relate to one another. What's more—our wandering had gone on for far too long. Across racial and class lines, we had come up with our own standards for how we should treat each other, and it had not done us any good.

As we saw in the passage we just read, God will occasionally allow unrest in order to urge His people to a heartfelt call on Him for help. He has to let His people hit rock bottom in order that we might discover He truly is the Rock at the bottom. Sometimes it takes a mess to make a miracle.

What are some ways God purges us as individuals and collectively of sinful toxins permeating this world?

List three sins or cultural problems that need to be purged from our culture today in order to be replaced by God's rule:

1.

2.

3.

What can be done to help remove these problems and replace them with the truth of God's Word and the healing power of His love?

Problems abound in our world today. We certainly have plenty for God to say, "Enough is enough!" But if we miss the reality that God has allowed disorder in order to bring about a correction and a cleaning, then we will just move from one symptom to another symptom. We will miss the opportunity to address the root that has produced the fruit that has led to the confusion of hopelessness on display.

The root of the problems we face in our churches, culture, and country today are clearly spiritual. To repair and restore our culture, we must understand the spiritual components behind our problems before proposing solutions to these crises.

To briefly examine one problem among many, over the past several years, our national conversation has returned again and again to race and racism. Racism isn't a bad habit. It isn't a mistake. It is sin. The answer is not sociology, it's theology. As kingdom men, we need to be just as bold in speaking out against the sin of racism as other sins when we confront it in others. We must also be willing to examine our own hearts for areas of racism, resentment, anger, and division.

In what ways have we learned to dismiss racism rather than confront it (whether in conversations, jokes, exclusionary choices, etc.)?

List some practical things that can be done to be proactive about ridding our culture of racism.

Do you think God wants us to be proactive about ridding our culture of racism? Why or why not?

In addition to racism, what other cultural problems do we need to take a spiritual-driven approach to resolving? List the problems and a few steps to resolve them.

Pray about your personal perspective on racism and the division of the races or ethnicities in our nation. Ask God to reveal to you any areas where you may hold prejudice or pride in your heart, then ask His forgiveness if He does reveal any. Take a moment to think about the purpose and power of unity, then ask the Spirit to show you how you can be more intentional about combating and overturning disunity in your circles of influence.

DAY 3
THE GOSPEL AND RACE

There are two types of sin in Scripture, but most of us examine our actions based on only one type. When we do that, we fail to take account of our whole experience and become less able to deal with the root issues.

The first type of sin is called sins of commission. This is when we do something that is inherently wrong. Sins of commission are things like telling lies, stealing things that don't belong to us, or looking at a woman lustfully. But there is another type of sin which goes largely ignored. It's called the sin of omission.

Read James 4:17 and answer the following questions.

Therefore, to one who knows the right thing to do and does not do it, to him it is sin.
James 4:17

On a scale of 1-10, how aware were you of this type of sin (omission)?

1	2	3	4	5	6	7	8	9	10

less aware   more aware

Why do you think there is less emphasis on sins of omission?

In your experience, how aware are most people about sins of omission? Why are these sins easier to ignore?

Read Micah 6:8 and circle what the prophet Micah wrote the Lord calls us to do.

He has told you, O man, what is good;
And what does the LORD require of you
But to do justice, to love kindness,
And to walk humbly with your God?
Micah 6:8

How is failing to do what the Lord requires here a sin of omission?
List a few examples.

Most of us know the right things to do. Sin here isn't a knowledge problem, but an action problem. To use racism as an example, when someone says to me, "I'm not racist," I am glad to hear they feel that way, and I do hope it's true. But Micah 6:8 isn't about "not doing injustice." It isn't about not being a racist.

Micah 6:8 doesn't call us to "love justice." Neither does it call us to "affirm justice." This passage specifically calls us to *do* justice. In Hebrew, this word could be translated "make" or "manufacture." In other words, God is asking us to take action.

According to the Word of God, we are to actively "do justice." What are some
ways we can actively "do justice"?

What tangible step can you take this week to "do justice"?

How is doing justice related to loving mercy and walking humbly with God?

God has spoken on the issues at hand, and He has not stuttered. He has spoken about racism. He has spoken about systemic and individual injustices. He has spoken about classism. He has spoken about culturalism. He has spoken about equity, elitism, empathy, and more. Just read the Book of James. That's a great place to start to learn. God has spoken about all of these subjects, but until we align our hearts, thoughts, words, and actions underneath His overarching rule, we are living in sin.

Righteousness and justice can be defined in the following ways:

- Righteousness is the moral standard of right and wrong to which God holds people accountable based on His divine standard.
- Justice is the equitable and impartial application of God's moral law in society.

> *Righteousness and justice are the foundation of Your throne;*
> *Lovingkindness and truth go before You.*
> **Psalm 89:14**

Based on those definitions and these words from the psalmist, answer the following questions.

Why is it important to balance both righteousness and justice?

Do you naturally give more attention to one or the other? Explain.

Can you name a contemporary example of someone who successfully pursued righteousness and justice at the same time?

Who are some role models for you who have lived committed to both righteousness and justice?

God desires that we embrace both righteousness and justice. We are to do what is right, but we are also to stand up and speak out for others in need. These actions promote an atmosphere of justice for everyone. Far too often, we confuse "justice" as that which gives someone who has done wrong what he or she deserves. But when God refers to "justice" in this particular passage, He is speaking about ensuring that all people are treated fairly and equitably.

When we decide to stand together for what is right and just in society, we can make a difference. We can change the trajectory of our culture. We can influence others for good by advancing God's kingdom agenda on earth. We do this primarily through the spread of the gospel.

Unity isn't just about getting along; it's about getting things done. We'll never experience a movement of kingdom men rising in our nation until we have kingdom men relating to each other in the body of Christ in an authentic, mutually honoring manner. Racial reconciliation isn't about playing a video of an ethnic preacher to your white church on Sunday or vice versa, reading books on racism, or posing online. While those things are good, in and of themselves, they are not unity. Unity takes place when people join together with oneness of purpose. It is working together in harmony toward a shared vision and goal. Unity involves doing justice together, not just talking about it.

Pray for open doors to share the gospel with others. Take time to ask God for ways that you can be more proactive in "doing justice" within your circle of influence. Pray for your small group and ask for insight from the Holy Spirit on ways your small group can tear down the walls of racism in order to advance the love of God through the gospel of Christ to a world in need.

Then Joshua said to the people,
"Consecrate yourselves, for tomorrow
the LORD will do wonders among you."

JOSHUA 3:5

WEEK 6
SETTING THE STAGE

START

Welcome to group session 6 of *Kingdom Men Rising*.

Last week, we talked about the call for us to be unified. In the personal studies, we looked at the crucial aspect of race and racism.

What was one lesson you learned from Dr. Evans's teaching on race?

This week, we will be talking about important spiritual disciplines for kingdom men. As an illustration, take your group on a short field trip. Go to a different, unfamiliar room from the one you usually meet in, like a gym or fellowship hall if possible. Go to one side of the room and have the guys in the group go to another. Give them a small light source like a flashlight or match (if they are mature enough for matches). Then turn the lights off and instruct them to crawl across the room, navigating around any obstacles there, and find their way to you using only their small light source. Once everyone has made it, return to your normal meeting space.

Share a time when you have had to trust God though your circumstances might have been dark or overwhelming.

You will probably never forget the challenges of 2020. Yet despite all the hardships we encountered, God has revealed His faithfulness time and again throughout that troubling year and the years that have followed. Perhaps you're just now seeing the fruit of His faithfulness despite overwhelming circumstances. Perhaps you are still wondering why God allowed things to go down the way they did. Often, God uses our circumstances to set the stage to reveal His incredible faithfulness.

Today, we'll look at an event in the life of Israel where God asked His people to show up. He was setting the stage for them to take their place in the land that He had promised. All they needed to do was show up, prepare themselves, and follow His directions.

Ask someone to pray before watching the video teaching.

WATCH

Use this space to take notes during the video teaching.

MAN UP

Use the following questions to discuss the video teaching.

Read Joshua 3:5 together.

Then Joshua said to the people, "Consecrate yourselves,
for tomorrow the LORD will do wonders among you."
Joshua 3:5

Prior to Joshua leading the Israelites across the Jordan River and into the promised land, God asked him and the people to do something. He asked them to "consecrate" themselves. To "consecrate" means to dedicate something or someone to a special purpose, task, or service.

God asked that Joshua and the people of Israel dedicate themselves for one purpose—crossing the Jordan River. He asked them to focus. He asked them to prepare themselves—emotionally, spiritually, and physically—for what He was about to do for them and through them.

What might it look like for us to "consecrate" ourselves or set ourselves apart for God's purposes today?

How does God grow us as we prepare to serve Him?

The people of Israel would have to trust God to make it across the Jordan. That's why their preparation mattered. Israel was to set out across the Jordan River at the height of flood season. The water spilled over the banks, and the ground beneath the waters was muddy. God would need to perform two miracles in getting the Israelites across the river. He would need to stop the waters from flowing, but He would also need to dry up the land enough for them to cross.

Imagine standing on the shores of the river knowing that somehow, the next day, you and thousands of people, animals, carts, and belongings would need to cross. What do you think the Israelites were thinking the day before they were to cross the Jordan River? What reasons did they have to be confident in God?

Life can get overwhelming sometimes. We get overwhelmed with tests, tryouts, practice of all sorts, college applications, relationships, and troubles within our famililies, church, or culture. We live in a flood zone, and often the flood is pouring over the banks. But during flood season, God is setting the stage for the supernatural to invade the natural to show us how big He really is. God allows flood season so that He can demonstrate that He alone is God.

How has God demonstrated to you that He alone is God during a difficult time in your life?

Only God could have performed the miracles necessary to get thousands across the Jordan River. He worked that way so that all the credit would be His. To remember what God had done, the Israelites took twelve stones from the Jordan River and placed them in their camp. All throughout Scripture, God called His people to remember what He had done and to share His work with others.

How can we better recognize that the opportunities we have are chances to witness God's strength and power in our lives?

How can we create a culture where we feel a greater need to focus on God and consecrate ourselves for the purpose of witnessing God's greater involvement in our circumstances?

Who needs to hear about how God has been faithful to you through a flood season? When will you set aside time to tell them?

PRAYER

Father, You have the power not only to dry up the waters which seek to overwhelm us, but You can also help us pass through the flood on the firmness of dry land. Help us to keep our eyes on You, stay focused on You, and consecrate ourselves to do the work of Your kingdom. In the name of Jesus, amen.

A PURPOSE-FILLED LIFE

Never measure God's movement without first taking a look at your own. God desires for us to move in obedience to Him before He makes His move. Whether it is Moses holding out the rod before He parted the sea or Peter crying out to Jesus before He rescued him from the storm, God frequently waits to see how we respond in faith before He fully reveals His hand in our lives.

In the story we are studying this week found in Joshua 3:7-17, the priests had to literally "walk by faith" before they would see God move. They had to put their feet in the water prior to God parting it for all to cross. Their example reveals three important principles we should all live by: listen, obey, and stand.

1
LISTEN

The priests had been asked to dedicate themselves for the specific task at hand—stepping into the flooding Jordan River. In order to do this, they needed to focus on what God said by consecrating themselves before Him. They wouldn't be able to hear Him if they had distractions in their lives at that time. We need to set aside distractions in our lives as well so we can better hear God in order to understand His instructions more clearly.

What have you heard from God recently?

OBEY

Stepping into the water of a river in order to get that same water to go away doesn't make a whole lot of sense. Yet that is what God asked the priests to do. Obeying God doesn't always involve us understanding His methods. Faith doesn't always make sense. But it can make miracles. Be willing to obey God when He makes your part in His plan clear to you.

How are you obeying based on what you've heard while listening to God?

STAND

And the priests who carried the ark of the covenant of the LORD stood firm on dry ground in the middle of the Jordan while all Israel crossed on dry ground, until all the nation had finished crossing the Jordan.
Joshua 3:17

We must never waver when called upon to serve God. From a human perspective, standing in the middle of what was previously a raging river isn't the safest place to be. But God doesn't call us to live safely; He calls us to live by faith. Sometimes that means standing strong where you are and in what you believe in so that those you love can get to where they need to go as well.

Why is it better to trust in God's power than in human limitations?

Father, I want to faithfully do these three things: listen, obey, and stand.
Empower me to live these three things out in my life. In the name of Jesus, amen.

DAY 2
LIFE ON LIFE DISCIPLESHIP

Developing strong muscles involves a process of tearing the fibers in your body in order to give your body the opportunity to produce muscle growth. The process of building muscles is painful because you cannot strengthen your muscles any other way.

Similarly, developing your spiritual muscles often comes during the difficulties and painful scenarios of life. That is when most of us will see the most growth, if we respond to our challenges rightly. If we choose to simply nurse our wounds and complain about the experience, we will not grow. It's only when we push through the pain that we'll discover growth on the other side.

Read Ephesians 1:11 and answer the following questions.

In him we have also received an inheritance, because we were
predestined according to the plan of the one who works out
everything in agreement with the purpose of his will.
Ephesians 1:11 (CSB)

Summarize this verse in your own words.

In what ways can God use pain and brokenness in agreement with the purpose of His will (see Rom. 8:28)?

What does it look like to develop your spiritual muscles? In what ways is that process painful?

Why must we grow to in order to help others?

We have obtained a spiritual inheritance from the Lord. But this inheritance is not only for us; it is for all who we come into contact with. To honor what we've been given, we must focus on our spiritual growth and development. It is the responsibility of every kingdom man, young and old, to take this inheritance and share it with others. This is the process of discipleship. It is the process where one takes the values of the kingdom and transfers them to another who will then transfer them to another.

This is our responsibility. This is what Abraham did with his son Isaac. What Elijah did with Elisha. What Jesus did with the Twelve. What Paul did with Timothy. We are to do nothing less, even if that means stepping out of your comfort zone. Standing for God will not always be popular, but it will always reap rewards.

Why is it often easier to go with the flow rather than speak up for God's truth?

When has following God called you to step out of your comfort zone? What did you learn?

Think of someone who impacted your own spiritual growth. Describe qualities about this person that stand out to you.

Discipleship takes boldness. Confidence. Love. Awareness. Commitment. Perhaps you used some of these traits to describe the person in the previous question. Difficult conversations on subjects of truth, sin, and redemption aren't easy. They require courage. People don't always want to hear the truth. Discipleship isn't necessarily fun, but neither are drills, conditioning, or weight lifting. Yet all of that is necessary to strengthen our muscles. Similarly, discipleship is necessary for us as young kingdom men. You're probably not in a place where you need to be teaching a class, but you need to be encouraging others with God's Word and setting an example to all with your speech, conduct, love, faith, and purity (see 1 Tim. 4:12).

Transferring kingdom values must take place on a regular basis through personal examples and authentic conversations about those examples. It's not done only through sermons, books, or podcasts. Those things are good, but they are supplemental. The transferring of kingdom values, as clearly outlined in Scripture, takes place person to person and heart to heart, like Paul instructed his young kingdom protégé, Timothy.

> *You therefore, my son, be strong in the grace that is in Christ Jesus. The things which you have heard from me in the presence of many witnesses, entrust these to faithful men who will be able to teach others also.*
> **2 Timothy 2:1–2**

Define "discipleship" based on the Scriptures above.

Who discipled you? Who can you help disciple?

If you have never been discipled, who is someone you can approach about helping you grow as a disciple?

At the root of all the issues we face in our nation, communities, churches, families, schools, and in our own individual lives is this lack of transference of kingdom values. Discipleship is a simple process, but it isn't easy. That's why we need to be strong in the grace Jesus gives. However, we can always be certain that the grace we need will always be supplied as we become more like Jesus.

Read Luke 6:40 and John 13:15 and answer the following questions:

> *A pupil is not above his teacher; but everyone, after he has been fully trained, will be like his teacher.*
> **Luke 6:40**

> *For I gave you an example that you also should do as I did to you.*
> **John 13:15**

Describe the cycle of discipleship based on these two verses.

Why is it sometimes tempting to leave the role of "discipleship" to those we consider to be "professional Christians" like pastors and small group leaders?

What should it teach us that Jesus's first disciples were ordinary men with no formal education?

Transferring kingdom principles doesn't only happen in small group settings in a classroom, although that is important. It comes through relationship, partnering, and doing life together.

Yet it seems that we often get so focused on weekly meetings or programs that we have forgotten this truth. We have forgotten what actually accomplishes the outcomes we desire and so desperately need—especially when you are standing on a riverbank staring at a raging river you have been asked to cross with everything you have.

The Israelites faced this river in Joshua 3. But we as men face our own rivers today. In order to rise up and cross through that which seeks to stop us, we are going to need to commit to this thing called "doing life together." We are going to need to embrace the call to kingdom discipleship on a deeper level.

Pray about anything in your life that may inhibit you from fully living out your call to be discipled and disciple others. Ask God to remove any obstacles in your way so that you can leave an impact on the lives of those around you. Be willing to embrace life's difficulties and pain as a way of growing spiritually, and spend some time seeking the Spirit's discernment on how you are to grow through the challenges you face.

DAY 3
TAKE A STEP. GRAB A STONE.

Read Joshua 4:1-24 before completing this study.

It's fun to get to see God show up in your life. It is in the times when He makes Himself real that our faith grows and we discover the satisfying feeling that comes with resting in God. But like a Super Bowl winning team who becomes too content with their victory, reveling in the past won't do a whole lot for your future. What's more, it won't do anything for anyone else's future either.

What would happen to a championship sports team who decided to focus more on the previous year's championship than on the next season?

Have you ever gotten a strong report card and then been tempted to slack off the next grading period? What kept you motivated to keep working hard? What was the result if you slacked off?

How can you guard yourself from falling into a similar slump after spiritual victory or success?

The crossing of the Jordan River was a tremendous miracle for Israel, on all fronts. But God didn't want the miracle to get lost in the enjoyment of its celebration. He knew that He needed to seed this miracle deep into the hearts and minds of the Israelites. He chose to do this by having them set up what we often call "stones of remembrance." These enormous stones would serve as a reminder to them about what God did to usher them into the promised land—providing a way when there was no way.

But God didn't have Joshua set up stones in just one place. One set of stones would remain in the middle of the Jordan River (see 4:9). The other would be set up at Gilgal, the city where Israel established its first camp (see 4:20). The stones served as a reminder, as well as a conversation-starter, for generations to come.

Why did God call Israel to set up stones in the middle of a river where no one would see them again?

Why does God ask us to continually remember what He has done for us?

"To this day"(v. 9) is a repeated phrase in Joshua. While we might not make monuments to God's faithfulness like the Israelites, what are some ways we can keep the work of the Lord in the front of our hearts and minds?

The stones placed in the river would be visible during the dry season as a reminder that, at one time, thousands crossed the dry river. The stones in the camp were a reminder to all who were at Gilgal. God did not want the Israelites to forget what He had done there for them. He didn't want them to forget where they came from and how they had gotten there. He had them set up a perpetual reminder that it was not by their might nor by their power that they had come this far. The twelve stones solemnly declared that they were there because of the supernatural hand of God.

"To this day" is a repeated phrase in the Book of Joshua. It was a signal for them to pause and remember the work of the Lord. God did this for the Israelites' good. He saw how quickly His people had forgotten the miracle of the ten plagues, the parting of the Red Sea, the food in the barren desert, and the water from a rock. He knew His people were prone to forgetfulness. So this time, He established a visible reminder of His sovereignty in the middle of their struggles.

Remembering who God is and what He has done is critical for each of us if we are to effectively grasp and one day transfer the principles of biblical manhood throughout the generations. That's one reason God emphasized this so much in Scripture.

Read the following verses and circle or underline any repeated concepts.

Only give heed to yourself and keep your soul diligently, so that you do not forget the things which your eyes have seen and they do not depart from your heart all the days of your life; but make them known to your sons and your grandsons.
Deuteronomy 4:9

Then it shall come about when the LORD your God brings you into the land which He swore to your fathers, Abraham, Isaac and Jacob, to give you, great and splendid cities which you did not build, and houses full of all good things which you did not fill, and hewn cisterns which you did not dig, vineyards and olive trees which you did not plant, and you eat and are satisfied, then watch yourself, that you do not forget the LORD who brought you from the land of Egypt, out of the house of slavery.
Deuteronomy 6:10–12

Beware that you do not forget the LORD your God by not keeping His commandments and His ordinances and His statutes which I am commanding you today.
Deuteronomy 8:11

Then your heart will become proud and you will forget the LORD your God who brought you out from the land of Egypt, out of the house of slavery.
Deuteronomy 8:14

But you shall remember the LORD your God, for it is He who is giving you power to make wealth, that He may confirm His covenant which He swore to your fathers, as it is this day. It shall come about if you ever forget the LORD your God and go after other gods and serve them and worship them, I testify against you today that you will surely perish. Like the nations that the LORD makes to perish before you, so you shall perish; because you would not listen to the voice of the LORD your God.
Deuteronomy 8:18–20

What are some of the recurring themes that show up in these passages?

What are some common outcomes which happen when we do "forget" God?

What processes do you have in place to remember what God has done?

How has God set the stage for your spiritual success lately?

God does miraculous work in His people's lives all of the time. But the problems arise when we forget what He has done and, as a result, either start taking the credit for ourselves or ignore His future guidance—or both. Setting up reminders of what God has done and how He has worked not only serves as a mechanism for our own personal spiritual stability and growth, but it also enables us to become better at sharing about the details of His power with others.

Take some time to think through ways you might want to memorialize events in your life where God has worked wonders. Pray and ask for the Spirit's guidance as you look to keep the memories of these breakthroughs fresh. Also seek God's hand and will for how you can better share about these testimonies in your life so that other people may become challenged to grow in their faith as well.

A good man leaves an inheritance
to his children's children,
And the wealth of the sinner
is stored up for the righteous.

PROVERBS 13:22

WEEK 7

FURTHERING THE FUTURE

START

Welcome to session 7 of *Kingdom Men Rising.*

Last session, we talked about how God sets the stage for our greatest spiritual victories and how He expects us to pass those blessings on through the process of discipleship.

> **Based on your personal study last week, what stones have you laid down to be reminded of what God has done in your life?**

This week, we will be talking about passing on to others what we believe and know about God. As an illustration, talk about a relay race and how a team only wins once they've successfully passed the baton to each team member and crossed the finish line. If you have space, let the guys in your group even try to pass a baton (or rolled up magazine, or whatever you can find) to each other like runners do in an Olympic race.

> **Why is it so important in a race to successfully pass the baton from one runner to the other?**

No matter how quickly you run in a relay, you will lose if you do not pass the baton. If you've ever watched an Olympic relay race, you've probably seen a team pull out in front only to come to a screeching halt when they fail to pass the baton from one teammate to the next and it drops to the track.

While we understand this principle when it comes to running relay races, we sometimes fail to grasp its importance when it comes to living as young kingdom men. A big part of our calling is to pass the baton to others. The world needs to know the truth and love of God in Jesus. We desperately need to realize this reality and rise up to fulfill this great purpose in the world today.

Ask someone to pray before watching the video teaching.

WATCH

Use this space to take notes during the video teaching.

MAN UP

Use the following questions to discuss the video teaching.

Read Proverbs 13:22 together.

A good man leaves an inheritance to his children's children,
And the wealth of the sinner is stored up for the righteous.
Proverbs 13:22

Kingdom men, young and old, are called to pass on a spiritual inheritance to others. While the Proverb we just read refers to one's direct descendants, the spiritual principle transcends family relationships. Anyone who is within your circle of influence ought to have a greater awareness of God and His kingdom values because of their relationship with you. Each of us pursues this goal differently, but we all share the same goal—transferring kingdom values to those around us.

To pass on kingdom values, we have to be aware of the spiritual needs of those around us and not just focused on ourselves. How can we condition our hearts to be aware of those around us and not just focus on our own needs?

Describe a time when you witnessed the successful transfer of kingdom values (whether to you from someone else or from you to someone else).

What happens if we don't make transferring kingdom values a priority?

All of you have different experiences with fathers. Some of your fathers are engaged and involved in your lives. Some of your fathers might not be. Regardless, if and when God calls you to be a father, it is your responsiblity to pass along kingdom values to your children. You might feel like this is something you don't have to worry about now because you are a teenager and years away from parenthood, but that couldn't be further from the truth. Remember in session 1 when we talked about foundations? This teaching is going into your foundation right now. If you believe it is your role now to pass on to others what God has taught you, you will do it for your children in the years to come when you are a parent.

Why do you suppose so many men don't pass on their faith to their children?

Read Deuteronomy 6:6-7 and answer the following questions.

*These words that I am giving you today are to be in your heart. Repeat them
to your children. Talk about them when you sit in your house and when
you walk along the road, when you lie down and when you get up.*
Deuteronomy 6:6-7 (CSB)

**What is God instructing the Israelites to do in these verses? When is He
instructing them to do it?**

These verses are part of what's called The Shema, which means "to hear." God was
telling the Israelites to hear clearly His instruction. He was telling them that it is the
role of parents to pass along to their children what they have seen, believe, and know
about God. And they are called to do it all the time—when they are stitting at home,
when they are going along the road, when they go to bed at night, and when they get up
in the moring. God is to be first and foremost on our hearts and minds.

If you take this seriously and do as God instructs in His Word, not only to your
children one day but to your circle of influence now, you will leave an undeniable mark
on this world for God and His kingdom. Small steps of discipleship lead to larger ones,
so don't worry about the fact that you are a teenager today. One day you won't be. Don't
wait until then to take this command from the Lord seriously. Start now.

How can you help impact others for God's kingdom today?

PRAYER

Father, in a world full of selfishness, You ask us to think of others
by investing in them through an intentional pursuit of spiritual
training. Enable us to identify those within our spheres of
influence who we can impact for Your kingdom and the greater
good of all involved. Open doors for us to have significant
influence on those we know and love. In Christ's name, amen.

DAY 1
HIT THE STREETS

FAMILY, FAITH, AND FAVOR

God has given us three distinct things to pass on to others. These three things are found in the blessing of the covenant. Passing these on won't happen just because you want it to happen. It will require your intentional engagement and pursuit.

FAMILY

Even as young kingdom men, we need to embrace family on every level. We need to be like a city set on a hill, displaying the light that comes from a fully functioning family. Whether that means modeling and mentoring the role of son, grandson, brother, cousin, nephew, and one day father, uncle, and grandfather—family roles should be taken seriously and honored. We do this by living authentically within each role, being responsible for what needs to be done. At this stage in your life, the greatest way you can do this is to live by Exodus 20:12: "Honor your father and mother."

FAITH

We are to be men of faith. To be a man of faith means that you allow your decisions to come underneath the rule of God in every area of your life. We sometimes confuse acting on faith to be leaps in the dark. While we don't know everywhere God will lead us, we are never in the dark. His Word is a light to our path (see Ps. 119:105). The man who walks consistently with God exhibits the greatest faith. Faith involves placing God's will for your life above your own will and desires. When you do that, you will not only demonstrate what a kingdom man of faith looks like, but you will also be investing in the faith of others as well.

FAVOR

Kingdom men recognize the difference between personal gain and God's blessing. God's blessing comes from His hand; great peace is found within it. Proverbs puts it like this:

It is the blessing of the LORD that makes rich,
And He adds no sorrow to it.
Proverbs 10:22

Divine favor is a key aspect of the blessing because God alone is able to supply all that a person needs. When you learn to rest in God's favor, you will also be positioned to teach others how to do the same. But as long as you are striving after your own personal success apart from God's leading in your life, you will be dropping the baton of favor which is yours to pass to others.

A kingdom man always focuses on the majors: family, faith, and favor. When these three things are flowing according to God's plan for your life, you will impact others and future generations for Christ.

How are you thankful for the family, faith, and favor God has given you?

How are you living out these three elements in your life today?

Father, regardless of the family I come from, I give my future family to You. Help me to honor Your plan for family and grow into a man of faith within my own family. Thank You for Your favor and love. In the name of Jesus, amen.

DAY 2
A LEGACY OF LOVE

You've likely seen the word "legacy" attached to sports, athletes, business owners, employees, volunteers, mentors, coaches, friends, and more, because it's all about passing down the DNA of greatness. These principles apply to all of us in the body of Christ, too. Legacy involves your impact on others. It's the spiritual DNA you pass down.

The question each of us must ask is: What kind of legacy am I leaving?

Read Genesis 1:28 and answer the following questions.

> *God blessed them; and God said to them, "Be fruitful and multiply, and*
> *fill the earth, and subdue it; and rule over the fish of the sea and over the*
> *birds of the sky and over every living thing that moves on the earth."*
> **Genesis 1:28**

This verse is God's commission to Adam and Eve. He gave them the command to populate the world and take ownership and care of the whole earth. Implied in this command is that Adam and Eve would care for their offspring as well by teaching them to obey God's command.

How did Adam obey this commandment in the garden of Eden?

How do we obey it in the situations where God has placed us?

How would our world look different if more of us saw the world as a place for us to take care of for the Lord today?

Every human being is an image-bearer. Being made in God's image means that every person is like God in ways that other created beings are not. We have souls and the capacity for reason and relationships. We are creative and industrious, like God.

Adam left the garden, but every kingdom man has the same commission as Adam—to fill the world with people who know and love God. To be about the work of passing on the spiritual inheritance of a kingdom world view.

Two predominant grids operate on this earth: humanism and theism. Humanism focuses what on mankind wants, thinks, and determines. Functioning according to humanism is like putting on sunglasses that focus only on what each person wants. Conversely, theism filters everything through the lens of God's perspective.

As kingdom men, we are created and called to transfer a theistic viewpoint to those within our circles of influence. In this way, we live out the DNA of the command God gave us when He created the world and left us in charge in Genesis 1:28.

What are the differences between humanism and theism?

In what ways does humanism bleed into our Christian culture?

Why do you think so many people consider humanism an acceptable grid to live by?

Adam wasn't commissioned to fill the earth with an accumulation of accolades, achievements, and material wealth. God called Adam to fill the earth with His image. A divine inheritance isn't about houses, clothes, cars, fame, or money. Divine inheritances start with the transfer of the faith. It doesn't matter how much money we have if we do not have the foundation of a solid faith. Without biblical values, it will all come crashing down when the storms of life roll in.

How do biblical values and a solid faith help a person, family, or community during difficulties in life?

What are some of the common difficulties we are facing as young men in our world today?

In what ways can we seek to infuse biblical values into the solution steps of these issues?

Many of us know we ought to live passionately for God's kingdom but aren't clear on what that means. Thankfully, when Christ came to fulfill the commandments, He gave us one summary commandment in place of all of them. This is what it means to follow God. Furthering the future means obeying this command and training others to do the same thing.

> One of them, a lawyer, asked Him a question, testing Him, "Teacher, which is the great commandment in the Law?" And He said to him, "'You shall love the LORD your God with all your heart, and with all your soul, and with all your mind.' This is the great and foremost commandment. The second is like it, 'You shall love your neighbor as yourself.' On these two commandments depend the whole Law and the Prophets."
>
> **Matthew 22:35-40**

Jesus told us that if and when we choose to love, we are fulfilling the commandments. Love is compassionately and righteously pursuing the well-being of another. Thankfully, Scripture helps us out here as well. Consider this biblical definition of love.

> Love is patient, love is kind and is not jealous; love does not brag and is not arrogant, does not act unbecomingly; it does not seek its own, is not provoked, does not take into account a wrong suffered, does not rejoice in unrighteousness, but rejoices with the truth; bears all things, believes all things, hopes all things, endures all things.
>
> **1 Corinthians 13:4-7**

Far too often, we relegate 1 Corinthians 13:4-7, a passage which describes love, as a wedding section of the Bible. While these verses apply to marriages, they also apply to everything we are to do and be. Let's take a look at them, but this time through the lens of biblical manhood.

How would emphasizing love positively impact our homes, schools, teams, communities, churches, and society?

What thoughts or hurdles tempt you away from responding to life's difficulties or relational issues with love?

How can we make the qualities of love more prevalent in society?

The greatest men in the kingdom of God understand love ought to be the way we roll with everyone. Sometimes, we may get so hung up on the emotional aspects associated with the term that we fail to understand what love truly means. Love should be the default posture of our hearts and lives. It is who God is and who we ought to be.

What are some of the ways we can model the qualities of love found in 1 Corinthians 13?

How might you specifically model this type of love?

Pray and ask God to nurture and strengthen the 1 Corinthians 13 qualities of love in your life so that you are better prepared to help others live out these qualities. Spend some time searching Scripture to better describe these qualities in order to understand God's heart on each one.

DAY 3
WISDOM AND AUTHORITY

What we share with those around us is critical. Whether it is tangible, physical goods, or life lessons—a greater focus on what we pass on to others will help in raising up more kingdom men who impact culture. One of the most dynamic male relationships in Scripture gives us insight into the nature of this transfer. It took place between Moses and Joshua. When we study their relationship, we see that Moses transferred many things to Joshua, like insight on how to lead, experience in battle, as well as countless lessons on communicating with God. But one of the more important aspects transferred to Joshua from Moses was the "spirit of wisdom."

Keep in mind, the Bible does not say that Moses passed down wisdom to Joshua. It says he passed down the "spirit of wisdom," specifically by laying his hands on him. Let's take a look at the passage and then examine it through a few questions.

Read Deuteronomy 34:9.

> *Now Joshua the son of Nun was filled with the spirit of wisdom,*
> *for Moses had laid his hands on him; and the sons of Israel listened*
> *to him and did as the LORD had commanded Moses.*
> **Deuteronomy 34:9**

What was Moses laying his hands on Joshua meant to communicate?

What was the result of Joshua receiving the "spirit of wisdom"?

What are some ways we can be a part of this kind of wisdom transfer today?

Do you think it's even necessary to model it? Why or why not?

In the passage we just looked at, we see how Moses transferred the values and perspective of the kingdom of God through transferring the "spirit of wisdom" to Joshua. A transfer of kingdom values and perspective can be passed down in many ways and should be passed down to all, but when a person has matured to the point of leading others, it is also important to pass down other things, such as spiritual authority.

We first see Moses laying his hands on Joshua back in Numbers 27:23. Then it was to impart spiritual authority.

> *Then he laid his hands on him and commissioned him,*
> *just as the LORD had spoken through Moses.*
> **Numbers 27:23**

How do you know if you are ready to receive spiritual wisdom passed down to you from someone who is discipling you?

Moses wasn't quick to pass on this spiritual authority to Joshua. He knew that he needed to wait until the time was right. One of the worst things to do to a man is give him authority when he is not mature enough yet to handle it. This is probably where you are right now. You are maturing, but you are not fully mature yet. It's like when you eat a piece of fruit that is not quite ripe. If you try to eat it before it's ready, you won't enjoy the experience.

The transfer of spiritual authority comes when someone recognizes you are ready to lead and transfer your spiritual fruit to others. Because Joshua had been a faithful servant, he now received his turn to lead. Joshua, like Moses, would now represent the Lord to the people of Israel. Through his relationship with Moses and his pursuit of the Lord, he gained the wisdom and authority necessary to lead well.

What are some key identifiers you want to exhibit before being commissioned to lead others?

Have you ever experienced someone (or yourself) being given spiritual authority too soon? If so, what was the result?

Unfortunately, too many of us want to lead without serving first. We want the authority without surrendering. That's backwards. It's like wanting to be the starting quarterback without even knowing the playbook. This is one reason why we are witnessing a large number of Christian leaders burn out or become disqualified from the ministry over scandals or misuse of the power given to them. Many had been given leadership roles due to their charisma and giftedness without first learning to serve and having the character to match.

Joshua had matured to the point where the blessing of spiritual authority was now his. And because he had spent so much time under the tutelage of Moses, he was able to keep the same vision going, albeit in a different style. He had his own methods, but the core of the ministry remained the same.

> *All Israel with their elders and officers and their judges were standing on both sides of the ark before the Levitical priests who carried the ark of the covenant of the LORD, the stranger as well as the native. Half of them stood in front of Mount Gerizim and half of them in front of Mount Ebal, just as Moses the servant of the LORD had given command at first to bless the people of Israel. Then afterward he read all the words of the law, the blessing and the curse, according to all that is written in the book of the law. There was not a word of all that Moses had commanded which Joshua did not read before all the assembly of Israel with the women and the little ones and the strangers who were living among them.*
> **Joshua 8:33-35**

How did Joshua's ministry model Moses's ministry?

Based on our study of Joshua, what are the critical elements someone needs in order to be discipled?

You need to be discipled yourself. You need to be trained in wisdom and spiritual authority. Who might disciple you? Have you considered asking them?

Pray about ways God would make you ready to receive spiritual wisdom and spiritual authority. Ask God to help you identify someone who can disciple you to a greater level. Ask Him to reveal the areas you most need to grow and develop in, then seek to pursue that spiritual growth yourself.

So then we pursue the things
which make for peace and the
building up of one another.

ROMANS 14:19

WEEK 8
IDENTIFYING KEY INFLUENCERS

START

Welcome to group session 8 of *Kingdom Men Rising.*

Last session, you were asked about how to implement small steps of discipleship into your daily rhythms. Let's talk about this for a minute.

As you considered ways to expand your spiritual influence, what incremental steps did you take?

This session, we will look more intently at how to identify key influencers. As an illustration, find two small presents and wrap them up like a birthday gift. In one, place a gift of modest value, like a $10 gift card to a fast food resturant. In the other, place something of no value, like a dead bug or a broken pencil. Randomly select a student in a fair way (like the closest guess to a number you choose), then let them pick which present they want. If they pick the bad one, give them the good one anyway.

What would happen to someone who consistently made bad decisions?

Decisions matter. Choices matter. God has given each of us the opportunity to live with what is known as "free will." Free will simply means that we have the ability to choose between potential courses of action without obstruction, yet inherent in each choice is an outcome. You were free to choose either present, you just didn't know what would be inside of them.

If you choose to walk down the middle of a busy road, you may get hit by a car. However, what we forget to teach others through discipleship is the importance of personal responsibility. We get bad outcomes through bad choices, and choices are made as we exercise free will.

Becoming a kingdom man means making the connection between our choices and outcomes and showing others the importance of this critical truth. Understanding this principle is essential in identifying potential influencers of the future.

Ask someone to pray before watching the video teaching.

WATCH

Use this space to take notes during the video teaching.

MAN UP

Use the following questions to discuss the video teaching.

How do our choices demonstrate that we are serious about influencing others?

On the other hand, how does making poor choices limit our influence?

Have you ever noticed that when one player on a sports team starts playing at a higher level, others rise with him? His standard of excellence and commitment rubs off on those around him and, as a result, the rest of the team plays better as well. Life as a kingdom man rising takes the same posture.

To be a kingdom man is to be an influencer. Life is no longer about yourself, but how you can bring others along. For a kingdom man to leave a spiritual heritage, he has to identify key influencers.

Read Romans 14:19 together and answer the following questions.

So then we pursue the things which make for peace
and the building up of one another.
Romans 14:19

What does it look like for us to "build up one another"?

Why is pursuing peace an important part of strengthening others in their walk with the Lord?

How does being contentious and argumentative hinder our ability to have an influence on others?

Sometimes we can confuse the bravado we seek to exude with actual strength. But bravado in and of itself often lacks true strength. Any time contention, boasting, or selfishness show up as a dominant force in our lives, division is the natural result.

In order to be an influencer who impacts others for good, we must first control our own character and align it under God's rule of love. Feeding our desire to be on top or have our ego puffed up is one of Satan's number one strategies for limiting the potential positive impact of influence that we can have in the lives of others.

Besides leading us to be contentious, what are some ways we can outmaneuver Satan in his attempts to keep us from rising as kingdom influencers?

How do accountability relationships and authentic conversations serve to keep us grounded in humility and truth?

Are you willing to have those difficult conversations with other guys or allow them to have them with you when things have gotten off track? Why are these essential? Why are these conversations not opposed to being peaceful?

Kingdom men, young and old, are serious about extending their influence. Influence comes through a number of ways. It could be setting an example. It could be through honest conversations. It might be through being willing to admit mistakes and correct them. Whatever the approach, keep in mind that influencing others for good involves making right choices as well as living with a spirit of biblical love. A leader not only tells the way, but he also shows the way through his own life, words, and behavior.

As this is our last session together, share one or two key truths you've learned through this study that you hope to put into practice.

What is one way the guys in this group can be praying for you as you seek to influence others?

PRAYER

Father, help us to make right choices so that we can be better positioned to influence others for Your glory and the advancement of Your kingdom. Show us what we need to do in order to help others understand Your will for their lives and rise to become influencers themselves. In the name of Jesus, amen.

HIT THE STREETS

THREE QUALITIES OF A KINGDOM INFLUENCER

Many qualities make up a person of influence, but there are three key traits that can help you either spot a future influencer or help develop one by focusing on these areas: character, competence, and commitment. When we are solid in all three of these areas, we will lead well by example and influence those around us.

1 CHARACTER

In order to be a kingdom influencer, we must have personal character. Take a moment to read Acts 6:3 and 1 Timothy 3:8-13. These verses speak to the character qualities of a deacon but, by default, a deacon was to be a man of influence. Thus, these qualities also transfer to kingdom men who seek to influence others. You are not old enough to be a deacon in your church, but you are never too young to be concerned about and focused on your character.

2 COMPETENCE

You may have heard it said that volunteers often have more heart than skill. They might mean well but wind up causing issues in whatever it is they are volunteering at due to a lack of competence in the role. Being an influencer is also about identifying ways we can develop a greater competence in all that we do. Psalm 78:72 gives us an example of both when it says of David:

> *So he shepherded them according to the integrity of his heart,*
> *And guided them with his skillful hands.*
> **Psalm 78:72**

3
COMMITMENT

Character and competence are only as good as the commitment behind them. If an NFL team were to draft a highly skilled player only to have that player quit after a few weeks, they would be worse off than before they chose him. Commitment is that quality which ensures that character and competence have the atmosphere to do their work. Commitment is lacking in our culture today. A lack of commitment negatively impacts everyone in its path. As young men seeking to be kingdom influencers, we must merge character with competence and commitment if we are truly going to leave a lasting impact during our time on earth.

Which of these three qualities do you need to cultivate most in your life?

What are some steps you'll take to cultivate this over the next month?

Father, as I continue to grow and mature, help these three qualities to increase in me as well. Help me to be a man of character. Let my yes be yes and my no be no. Help me to grow in my competence. As I learn and develop, let my abilities also become greater for the sake of Your kingdom. Finally, let my commitment to you never waver. Help my heart be concerned for and connected to the things you love the most—Your church and the family. In the name of Jesus, amen.

DAY 2
INFLUENCING INFLUENCERS

You can measure the destiny of a team—whether that be a family, school group, sports team, church, community, or even a nation—by its leadership. Unfortunately, today we face a crisis of leadership. People don't know who to follow anymore because this crisis has produced so many poor models and mentors and an utter lack of great leaders.

Yet, God's kingdom program is designed around the process of transferring spiritual wisdom, known as discipleship, in order to produce future leaders. One of the primary roles of kingdom men is to lead others in the way they should go. God has called us to be leaders. The issue is whether we will be great leaders or poor ones.

Read the following passages and write down how each passage describes biblically-based kingdom leadership.

Titus 1:7-9

1 Timothy 4:12

Hebrews 13:7

Matthew 10:42-45

Galatians 6:9

John 13:34-35

Steadfastness, kindness, love, faith, self-control, dignity, teachability, hospitality, and a love for God's Word are some qualities that contribute to making a great leader.

What are some cultural and secular traits that we often look for in influencers?

In what ways do these differ from the biblical traits listed in the previous verses?

One of the biggest mistakes people make in raising up future leaders is the assumption that great leadership is only taught, not caught. What this means is that people we seek to influence learn about us more from what they see out of us than what they hear us say. We are best able to influence organically and authentically when we share our lives, experiences, and conversations with each other.

Becoming a key influencer means we learn to solidly speak on biblical truths and navigate the storms of society. This requires guidance, practice, learning, and listening. Just like any team is dependent on everyone contributing for it to be great, becoming a kingdom influencer requires us to put forth the effort to learn, grow, listen, be taught, discern, practice, model, and more.

What would need to change in your life to make room for more relationships that can help you grow as well as help others to grow, too?

On a scale of 1-10, how important is it to increase this level of engagement?

1	2	3	4	5	6	7	8	9	10
Not Important								**Very Important**	

As leaders pour into us, we will grow in our leadership abilities. Coaching trees in the NFL are a great example of this principle at work. The best coaches have multiple assistant coaches who go on to coach teams themselves. You can judge a coach, at least in part, by their coaching tree. In the spiritual realm, kingdom men carry the same capacity to influence others and raise others up who will make a difference in the world for Christ.

What are some critical elements that make a coaching tree successful at developing future great coaches?

How can we apply some of these elements to our relationships and systems so that we can have a greater collective impact on our society?

Let's be clear. You are not here just for you. You are here for others. You have been crafted and created by God as an instrument of influence for the furthering of His kingdom agenda on earth. Satan has done a great job of getting men, young and old, to focus on the areas of life which do not lead to generational transfer of kingdom values. But it is time that we rise up as men to take our stand against the enemy's schemes. Paul gave us wisdom for how to accomplish this purpose in 2 Corinthians.

> *For although we live in the flesh, we do not wage war according to the flesh, since the weapons of our warfare are not of the flesh, but are powerful through God for the demolition of strongholds. We demolish arguments and every proud thing that is raised up against the knowledge of God, and we take every thought captive to obey Christ.*
> **2 Corinthians 10:3-5 (CSB)**

How can we do a better job collectively to "demolish arguments and every proud thing that is raised up against the knowledge of God" (v. 5)?

Have you ever blindly trusted a friend only to later discover he led you down the wrong path? Describe the role of discernment when it comes to identifying and maintaining accountability and growth-based relationships.

Where do you think our culture could wind up if an army of kingdom men were to rise up for righteousness, justice, and the advancement of God's Word?

Satan tries to get us to forget that we do not wage the battle for influence and leadership in our culture with worldly weapons. We wage this battle through the power of the Spirit and by using weapons He provides. One of the primary weapons is the wisdom needed to discern truth from Satan's lies. As we do that, we will see how important it is to help others to do the same. Satan uses deception as a primary tool in keeping us held back from living as the leaders we have been designed to be.

Pray about ways you can both better discern God's role and leading in your life and how you need to grow, as well as how you can live with greater kingdom influence on those around you. As God brings ideas to your mind, ask Him to open the doors and show you the way on how to pursue them. Let Him know you are willing to be used by Him to positively impact the lives He brings within your circles of influence.

DAY 3
KINGDOM DECLARATION

Without a doubt, we face a culture that wants to trick us, trip us up, and get us to make the wrong decisions in this life. But the answer to whether we will experience spiritual victory in our walk is in our own hands. Satan only appears to be winning this war. It's not because Satan is more powerful; Satan is not more powerful than Christ.

If we choose to follow Christ by cultivating a relationship with Him and submitting to His rule, we will defeat the enemy at every turn. Any other path we pursue will result in further destruction. The choice is ours to make. The time to make that choice is now.

It is high time we rise up as one voice and one example for each other, our friends, our churches, our schools, and our communities. We know the One who knows how this story ends. We know the One who knows the end from the beginning. The One who crafted and created us has already determined that His purposes WILL be carried out.

Read Isaiah 46:10 and answer the following questions:

Declaring the end from the beginning, and from ancient times things which have not been done, saying, "My purpose will be established, and I will accomplish all My good pleasure."
Isaiah 46:10

In what ways can you participate more fully in pursuing the carrying out and accomplishing all of God's "good pleasure"?

Describe what you feel knowing that God's purposes will be established.

Take time to examine your life and choices based on what you have learned in this study. Then, take a moment to write out your own prayer to conclude this time of study. Focus on what you are grateful for and what you would like to see improved in your own life and in the lives of those you love through your influence.

Dear God, _____

D-GROUP GUIDE

If you're reading this, you likely care about discipleship. You desire to be a kingdom man living under God's kingdom agenda. Being in a small group or a Sunday School class is one means believers use to go deeper in the Christian life. However, increasingly, people want closer and more tight-knit community. To this end, we've provided a guide to facilitate those kinds of small groups.

WHAT IS A D-GROUP? As opposed to an open small group or a Sunday School class (meaning everyone is welcome), a D-Group is a closed group that three or four people join by invitation and are committed to.

WHAT'S THE PURPOSE OF A D-GROUP? These groups are for Christians who desire to walk more closely with the Lord. The smaller nature of the group allows a more concentrated level of accountability and opens up discussions that are more personal than in a standard group meeting.

WHY DO I NEED A D-GROUP? We're not meant to live the Christian life alone. You'll need support as you seek to live as a kingdom man. Opening yourself up to people in a smaller environment encourages participation from you and from those who may not feel comfortable opening up in a larger group.

Additionally, D-Groups give others permission to speak into your life for encouragement, accountability, and prayer.

WHAT'S REQUIRED OF ME? The goal of these groups is deeper discipleship and accountability. Achieving this goal requires commitment. Plan to meet for one hour. Be willing to attend and participate each week. Be willing to be open and honest about your spiritual condition and about ways you're struggling. Be willing to hold what's said in the group in confidence. What's said should remain in the group as a means of building trust with one another. Finally, be willing to pray and support one another. Allow the relationships to extend beyond the group meeting itself.

HOW TO USE THESE GUIDES

A D-Group guide is provided for each week of this study. These guides are meant to be used in addition to the weekly group session, but can be also used by people who aren't meeting with a group. However, these guides work best if participants have seen the week's video teaching. Each D-Group guide includes the following elements.

SUMMARY. Summary of key ideas from the session.

D-GROUP QUESTIONS. These open-ended questions are designed to encourage the guys in your group to open up about their struggles and successes for the purposes of growth and accountability.

SESSION 1
CHOSEN FOR THE CHALLENGE

SUMMARY

As a young kingdom man, God has given you a purpose to live out and a divine design to fulfill. This session speaks to your unique calling to provide the foundational framework upon which your influence can rest and rise.

KEY QUESTIONS

Do you feel chosen by God for the challenge of being a kingdom man? Why or why not?

What are some ways you can embrace the calling to be a young kingdom man every day?

How can intentional friendships cultivated in groups like this keep us accountable and on track to stay focused on the challenge ahead?

Share some expectations you have for the other guys in the group.

SESSION 2
DRY BONES DANCING

SUMMARY

Some guys are held back because they are unable or unwilling to overcome Satan's distractions and trust in God's plans, purposes, and promises. However, God can take a stale or declining spiritual life and give it renewed vitality.

KEY QUESTIONS

Share which of Satan's distractions you are most prone to follow.

What are a couple of ways we can hold each other accountable and help each other refocus on God?

Describe your current proximity to God. How is He giving you spiritual vitality?

What is a promise of God you are focusing on this week? Explain.

SESSION 3
GET UP

SUMMARY

Sometimes life's difficulties knock us out, beat us down, or get us off the field completely. Standing up after you've been knocked down is rarely a solo experience. It takes others to come alongside you to lift you, encourage you, and strengthen you.

KEY QUESTIONS

Who has been a key encourager to you in your spiritual life? How can you be similarly encouraging to others?

Where do you need to "get up" and overcome spiritual lameness?

Review the steps on pages 46-47. Which one is most helpful to you right now? Where could you stand to grow?

Is there a guy you know who needs to "get up" and take hold of his spiritual health? How can you help him?

SESSION 4
GET GOING

SUMMARY

Too many of us today have identified with too many false gods. We need to step up, get going, and move away from the lifeless idols robbing us of spiritual vitality and impact. When we put away our idols and embrace God's better plan for our lives, He will use us to do something bigger than what we could have ever done on our own.

KEY QUESTIONS

What are the most common idols that plague us today? Where do you see these in your friendships or in the world around you?

When might guys need help moving away from idols? Why should we help other guys see this need?

Recall the story of Gideon from this week's study in Judges 6. How did God alter Gideon's identity? Where does God need to shape your identity?

How do healthy spiritual habits break us from idols? What habits do you need to cultivate?

SESSION 5
GET ALONG

SUMMARY

Much of the chaos and defeat we are experiencing today is a result of disunity among each other. The divisions in our world need kingdom men, young and old, who will rise and lead, displaying unity through all we say and do.

KEY QUESTIONS

Why do you think demonstrating love for one another reveals to others that we are Christ's kingdom disciples?

How can we be guys who contribute to harmony and peace instead of division?

Is there any area of your life where you are pursuing division instead of unity? What changes do you need to make?

What does it look like to be a young kingdom man who preserves and pursues kingdom unity?

SESSION 6
SETTING THE STAGE

SUMMARY

Far too often, God is waiting on us to obey Him before He will make His move. Whether it is Moses holding out the rod before He parts the sea or Peter calling out to Jesus before He rescues him from the storm—God frequently waits to see how we respond in faith before He fully reveals His hand in our lives.

KEY QUESTIONS

Where might you need to embrace God's faithfulness and follow Him?

Why is it so easy for us to get overwhelmed in "flood" seasons? What steps can we take to depend on God and keep our heads above water?

Where do you need to listen to stand and obey God?

Why is it better to trust in God's power than in human limitations?

SESSION 7
FURTHERING THE FUTURE

SUMMARY

Part of being a kingdom man is the successful passing on of kingdom values. The buck doesn't stop with you. We desperately want others to realize this and rise up to fulfill this great purpose in the body of Christ today. We further the future by being discipled and passing the gift of discipleship to others.

KEY QUESTIONS

Read Proverbs 13:22. What does this look like in your life? As guys without children yet, how can you impact the next generation?

To pass on kingdom values, we have to think about others and not merely be personally fulfilled. Describe the differences between thinking about others as opposed to only being personally fulfilled. Which are you? Explain.

Discuss ways that each of you in the D-group can add small, yet intentional, steps of discipleship to your normal routine.

What has the previous generation passed on to you?